# A General Introduction to the Bible

## Chas. P. Grannan

Copyright © BiblioLife, LLC

This book represents a historical reproduction of a work originally published before 1923 that is part of a unique project which provides opportunities for readers, educators and researchers by bringing hard-to-find original publications back into print at reasonable prices. Because this and other works are culturally important, we have made them available as part of our commitment to protecting, preserving and promoting the world's literature. These books are in the "public domain" and were digitized and made available in cooperation with libraries, archives, and open source initiatives around the world dedicated to this important mission.

We believe that when we undertake the difficult task of re-creating these works as attractive, readable and affordable books, we further the goal of sharing these works with a global audience, and preserving a vanishing wealth of human knowledge.

Many historical books were originally published in small fonts, which can make them very difficult to read. Accordingly, in order to improve the reading experience of these books, we have created "enlarged print" versions of our books. Because of font size variation in the original books, some of these may not technically qualify as "large print" books, as that term is generally defined; however, we believe these versions provide an overall improved reading experience for many.

# A GENERAL INTRODUCTION TO THE BIBLE

BY

THE RT. REV. CHAS. P. GRANNAN, D.D., Ph.D.

CONSULTOR TO THE PONTIFICAL BIBLICAL COMMISSION AND PROFESSOR
EMERITUS OF THE CATHOLIC UNIVERSITY OF AMERICA

*IN FOUR VOLUMES*

VOLUME IV

Biblical Hermeneutics—Biblical Exegesis

B. HERDER BOOK CO.
17 SOUTH BROADWAY, ST. LOUIS, MO.
AND
68, GREAT RUSSELL ST., LONDON, W. C.
1921

*NIHIL OBSTAT*

*Sti. Ludovici, die 7. Martii* 1921
*F. G. Holweck,*
*Censor Librorum.*

*IMPRIMATUR*
*Sti. Ludovici, die 8. Martii* 1921
☩*Joannes J. Glennon,*
*Archiepiscopus*
*Sti. Ludovici.*

*Copyright, 1921*
*by*
*Joseph Gummersbach*

*All rights reserved*
*Printed in U. S. A.*

(A GENERAL INTRODUCTION TO THE BIBLE)

## PREFACE

Instead of overwhelming the students with innumerable minute rules of grammar and logic (which will all come around in due time), the writer has endeavored to show on what a broad and deep and solid foundation both the divine authority and the correct interpretation of Sacred Scripture rest. With this end in view, he has rather fully explained what is meant by tradition, both in general and in some of its many varieties, and has shown its supreme importance, not only for fundamental dogmatic theology and for the Church, but also for the canon, for the divine inspiration, and for the doctrinal interpretation of Holy Scripture.

After all, what the young theologian needs more than all else, is an intimate and proper understanding of the fundamental questions regarding the human and the divine authority of our Sacred Books, and a clear insight into the mutual relations existing between the Catholic Church and divine tradition and Holy Scripture, on which depends also the Catholic principle of Biblical interpretation.

# CONTENTS

|  | PAGE |
|---|---|
| PREFACE | iii |

I. BIBLICAL HERMENEUTICS . . . . . . . . . . . . 1
    Introduction . . . . . . . . . . . . . . . 1
    The Object of Hermeneutics . . . . . . . . 1
    The Need of Hermeneutics . . . . . . . . . 1
    Definition of Hermeneutics . . . . . . . . . 2

PART I. THE SENSE OF SCRIPTURE IN GENERAL . . . . 7
    Preliminary . . . . . . . . . . . . . . 7
    A. The Literal Sense Single . . . . . . . 9
    B. The Typical or Mystical Sense . . . . . 11
    C. The Accommodated Sense . . . . . . 15

PART II. HOW TO DISCOVER THE SENSE OF SCRIPTURE . . 19
    Ch I. The Rational Principles of Hermeneutics . . 25
    The Biblical *Usus Loquendi* . . . . . . . . 26
    Figurative Language . . . . . . . . . . 27
      1. The Context . . . . . . . . . . . 29
      2. The Biblical Parallelism . . . . . . . 30
      3. The Subject Matter . . . . . . . . 31
      4. The Scope of the Writer . . . . . . 31
      5. The Occasion of Writing . . . . . . 32
    Ch. II. Christian Principles of Hermeneutics . . 35
    First Proposition: The Books of Scripture are to be interpreted in such a way as to admit no error in the words of the inspired writers . . . . . 36
    Second Proposition: Sacred Scripture is to be interpreted in such a way that no contradiction shall ever be admitted between the statements of inspired writers . . . . . . . . . . . . 41
    Ch III. Catholic Principles of Hermeneutics . . . 47
    The Direct or Special Method of Interpreting Sacred Scripture . . . . . . . . . . . . . . 49
    The Rules Laid Down by Trent . . . . . . 50

# CONTENTS

|  | PAGE |
|---|---|
| Third Proposition · In explaining passages of Scripture that pertain to faith and morals, the Catholic interpreter should follow "the sense which the Church has held and still holds." | 55 |
| Fourth Proposition: In explaining passages of Scripture that pertain to faith and morals, the Catholic interpreter must follow that sense which the Fathers have given with unanimous consent and settled conviction | 61 |
| Objections refuted | 65 |
| Fifth Proposition: The decree "Insuper" of Trent, containing the two preceding rules or propositions, is not only negative, but also positive in character and purpose | 67 |
| Seventh Proposition: In those doctrinal passages which have received no definite interpretation from either the Church or the Fathers, the Catholic interpreter should follow the analogy, not only of Biblical, but also of Catholic faith | 70 |
| Eighth Proposition · An obligation in conscience rests on all, without exception, to submit to the doctrinal decisions of the Pontifical Biblical Commission, whether promulgated in the past or in the future, just as all are obliged to submit to the decrees of the S. Congregations, when approved by the Pope | 77 |
| The Catholic Rule of Faith | 78 |
| Ch. IV. Protestant Principles of Interpretation | 83 |
| 1. First Protestant Principle of Interpretation | 84 |
| 2. Second Protestant Principle of Interpretation | 85 |
| Ch. V. Rationalistic Principles of Interpretation | 95 |
| 1. Socinianism | 95 |
| 2. Rationalism | 97 |
|    A. The System of Positive Dogmatic Accommodation | 102 |
|    B. The System of Moral Interpretation | 105 |
|    C. The System of Psychological or Naturalistic Interpretation | 107 |
|    D. The System of Mythical Interpretation | 108 |
|    E. The System of Legendary Interpretation | 112 |

## CONTENTS

| | PAGE |
|---|---|
| Ch VI. Divine Tradition an Essential Part of the Catholic Principle of Hermeneutics | 117 |
| Definition | 117 |
| Division | 118 |
| Divine-Ecclesiastical Tradition | 125 |
| Mutual Relations between Divine-Ecclesiastical Tradition and S. Scripture | 128 |
| The Catholic Doctrine of Tradition | 134 |
|     1. The Teaching of Scripture | 134 |
|     2. The Teaching of the Fathers | 137 |
|     3. The Teaching of Church History | 139 |
|     Protestant Objections Refuted | 153 |
|     The Place of S. Scripture in the Church | 154 |
|     Tradition the First Rule of Christianity | 162 |

PART III HOW TO EXPLAIN TO OTHERS THE SENSE OF SCRIPTURE . . . 171
Definition . . . 171
Kinds of Exegesis . . . 171
  1. Translation . . . 172
  2. The Paraphase . . . 173
  3. The Commentary in General . . . 174
    a) The Gloss . . . 174
    b) The Scholion . . . 175
    c) The Annotation . . . 176
    d) The Homily . . . 176
    e) The Exegetical Dissertation . . . 178
    f) The Commentary Proper . . . 179
    Requisites of a Good Commentary . . . 180
    Kinds of Commentary . . . 182
      1) Philological Exegesis . . . 183
      2) Theological Exegesis . . . 183
      3) Homiletical and Practical Exegesis . . . 185

APPENDIX. SOME RESULTS OF EXEGESIS . . . 189
  Biblical Theology . . . 189
  Biblical History . . . 189
  Biblical Biography . . . 190

BIBLIOGRAPHY . . . 195

ALPHABETICAL INDEX . . . 199

# BIBLICAL HERMENEUTICS

## INTRODUCTION

Have we sufficient acquaintance with the laws of language and thought among the ancient Hebrews to insure good results in an attempt to understand their writings? This question is discussed and solved in " Biblical Hermeneutics."

### *The Object of Hermeneutics*

Every literary composition, sacred as well as profane, consists of thoughts expressed in words, according to the laws of grammar, rhetoric and logic. The thoughts are the kernel, the words are the shell. It is the object of Hermeneutics to extract the one from the other.

### *The Need of Hermeneutics*

The necessity of Hermeneutics is apparent, even when reading works written by authors belonging to our own age, to our own country, to our own language, to our own civilization, and when writing on topics with which we are familiar. But when there is question of understanding a book like the *Bible*, written by many authors, living at irregular intervals, and scattered over a period of one thousand, five hundred years, and from two thousand to three thousand years ago, by Asiatics, under a form of Oriental civilization, in a language as different from the Indo-European family of languages, to which our own belongs, as one pole is from the other; composed of bits of poetry, hymns, canticles, and scraps of ancient history, often incomplete and fragmentary, and put together "at sundry times and diverse manners," in every kind of style of which human language is capable, and containing a record of revelation in which the thoughts of Heaven are expressed in the language of the sons of men; the necessity of the guiding principles of Hermeneutics becomes too apparent to need any attempt at demonstration

Briefly, the more remote the time, the more distant the place, and the more different the laws, customs, manners, language,— especially if it has been a dead language for the last two thousand years or more,— then, the greater is the need of some system of Hermeneutics in order to understand properly a book written in those far-off circumstances.

## Definition of Hermeneutics

Biblical Hermeneutics may be defined as the *science* and the *art* of discovering the sense of Sacred Scripture and explaining it to others. As a science, it consists of broad, general, abstract principles, based on grammar, rhetoric and logic. As an art, it consists of detailed, practical, concrete rules, the result largely of experience.

The *purpose* of Hermeneutics, as is evident from this definition, is three-fold, namely, to show:

(1) What is meant by the *sense* of Scripture in general;

(2) How to *discover* the sense of Scripture;

(3) How to *explain* to others the sense of Scripture.

# PART I
# THE SENSE OF SCRIPTURE IN GENERAL

# PART I

# THE SENSE OF SCRIPTURE IN GENERAL

### PRELIMINARY

The sense of a writing is the "*mens auctoris,*" the mind of the author. In other words, the sense of a writing is that thought which the author had in mind and which he wishes to communicate to others by means of his book, by his written language.

When the reader remembers that the principal Author of Scripture is the Holy Spirit of God, and that the inspired writer is only the secondary author, it will be manifest that the sense of Scripture is primarily the meaning which the Holy Ghost wishes to communicate to us through the language of the inspired writer. This fact of the divine authorship of Scripture helps us to realize how it is that beneath the surface of the sacred text many a mysterious meaning is hidden and can be discovered only by study and meditation.

In fact, Sacred Scripture is the only book in existence, in some parts of which there are *two different* kinds of sense, and both kinds intended by the Author.

The first is called the *Literal* and

The second is called the *Mystical* sense

## I. THE LITERAL SENSE

The literal sense is expressed directly and immediately by the *words* of the text, when taken in either their proper literal, or in their improper literal, or metaphorical sense. *E. g.,* " God created heaven and earth." The literal sense is also often called the direct, immediate, historical or verbal sense.

The *mystical* or *typical* sense is expressed, not immediately by the words, but by the *thing, event* or *person,* which, in turn, is expressed by the words. But of this later on.

The literal sense is sub-divided chiefly into two kinds or varieties, (a) the proper literal sense and, (b) the improper literal or the metaphorical sense.

a) The *proper literal* sense is expressed directly and immediately by the words, when taken in their *obvious, natural, ordinary* meaning; for instance: " I am the Lord Thy God "; " I and the Father are one."

b) The *improper literal* or *metaphorical* sense is expressed directly and immediately by the words, when taken in a *figurative* or *derived* sense, that is, when slightly turned aside or transferred from their usual meaning; for instance: " I am the vine "; " I am the door."

These two varieties of the literal sense are, of course, both literal, because both expressed by the *letter,*— both expressed directly and immediately by the *words* of the text.

There is this technical difference (not always observed) between " signification " and " sense ": *Sig-*

*nification* is the meaning of *separate, detached* words, *i.e.,* as found in the dictionary. There are always as many significations as words, and often more, for some words have many significations. *Sense* is the meaning of a *collection* of words, combined according to the rules of grammar in such a way as to form a sentence or a proposition. There is, or should be, only one sense in any sentence of any non-Biblical writers. In certain parts of Scripture we have exceptions to this rule.

### A) *The Literal Sense Single*

It is the common opinion of Catholic scripturists and theologians that there is *one,* and only one, literal sense, whether proper or metaphorical, in each and every passage of Sacred Scripture.

The reason is evident. If a passage of Scripture has no literal sense, then it has no typical sense, either; for, as St. Thomas says, the typical is based on the literal sense, pre-supposes it and can not exist without it.

If a passage of Scripture has neither a literal nor a mystical sense, then it has *no sense* at all, for there is no other kind than these two. In other words, the Holy Ghost speaks and says nothing,— which is absurd.

In the past, there have been some very distinguished theologians who maintained that (not all, but only) some passages of Sacred Scripture have several literal senses.

As this topic is complicated and easily misunderstood, a careful explanation of the point at issue will greatly facilitate the proof of the thesis, as follows:—

A passage of Scripture may have many senses *put upon it* by the interpreter, and all but one may be accommodated senses, which do not express the mind of the author.

Again, a passage of Scripture may be *ambiguous,* that is, it may have many merely *possible* senses or interpretations put upon it, and all literal; yet, only one of them is the *real sense intended by the author;* though we may not know for certain which is the true sense. For instance, " His generation, who shall relate it? " This passage has been variously interpreted by various writers. By some, it is understood of the *eternal* generation of the Word from the Father; by others, of His *temporal* generation from his mother; by others, of the generation of *wicked men* living in his time; by others, of the vast multitude of His *disciples* in all ages

This last is very probably the proper interpretation of the passage.

Again, a passage of Scripture may have many senses and all intended by the author; but *only one* at most is the literal, the others are mystical. The word Jerusalem in some of the Psalms, *e.g.,* 47 and 86, has four senses, all intended by the author; but three are mystical and only one is the literal sense. In the literal sense, Jerusalem is the capital city of Palestine; in the allegorical sense, it is the Church of Christ; in the tropological sense, it is the soul of the good Christian; in the anagogical sense, it is Heaven.

The word Jerusalem, when examined etymologically, is variously explained by various authors to mean either the "possession of peace" or the "abode of peace" or the "city of peace." Any of these meanings will suit the case.

Again, a passage of Scripture may *apparently* have many literal senses and all intended by the author; but they are all contained, as individuals in a species, or as species in a genus, or as effects in their causes, or as parts in a whole, or as conclusions in a premise, or as partial and incomplete statements are contained in, and so deducible from, one sweeping proposition. Yet, in all such cases there is only *one complete literal sense,* — the sense of the general proposition. "Wherefore, labor that by good works you make your vocation secure" (II Peter 1, 10). The phrase "good works" is equivalent to the corporal and to the spiritual works of mercy and includes good works of whatsoever kind.

B) *The Typical or Mystical Sense*

The *typical* or *mystical* sense is expressed, not immediately by the words, but immediately by the *thing, event* or *person,* which, in turn, is expressed by the words. The mystical sense is often called the typical, indirect, mediate, real, or spiritual sense.

St. Thomas says in substance: "It is in the power of God, not only to make words signify things, which we also can do, but also to make things signify other things, which we can not do. When words directly signify things, we have the literal sense. But, when the things signified by those words are in turn made to signify still other things, we have the typical sense; and this typical sense is founded upon and pre-supposes the existence of the literal sense and cannot exist without it."

There is always this one essential difference between the typical sense and the literal sense, whether proper or metaphorical: In the literal sense, whether proper or metaphorical, only *one* thing (event, rite, institution, person) is intended by the author; it is the thing which is expressed by the *words,* when taken in their proper literal, or in their improper literal or transferred sense.

When we say, " Christ is the vine, we are the branches," " Christ is the door to the sheepfold," we do not take the words *vine* and *door* in their obvious, ordinary, literal sense, but in their figurative or transferred sense. We do not mean that Christ is a real vine growing in the field and clinging to a trellis; we do not mean that Christ is a real door made of boards swinging on hinges and fastened with lock or latch, with bar or bolt. In the metaphorical sense of the words *vine* and *door,* Christ is to His disciples, in the spiritual order, what the vine is to its branches and what the door is to those who pass through it in the natural order,— support and access. The thing that could be expressed by the word, if taken in its strictly literal sense, is not so intended and often could not possibly be so intended, by the author.

On the other hand, in the typical or mystical sense, *two* things are presented to the mind. We read, for instance, " Take a male lamb one year old without spot

## THE TYPICAL OR MYSTICAL SENSE 13

or blemish . . . and sacrifice it in the evening" (Exodus 12, 5).

The first object presented to the mind of the reader in this text is the Hebrew paschal lamb, sacrificed according to the Aaronic ritual.

The second object presented to the mind is the Christian Paschal Lamb, foreshadowed by the Hebrew paschal lamb.

Now, both these things, that is to say, both these lambs are true, both are historical facts, and both are at the same time intended by the author, but expressed in different ways.

The sacrifice of the Hebrew paschal lamb, as described in Exodus 12, 5, ff., actually took place every year with great pomp and ceremony, for a period of more than 1000 years, and was specially ordained by God to typify or to foreshadow the death of Christ for the people. This is evident from the following and many other passages: "Christ, our pasch, is sacrificed" (I Corinthians 5, 7). "[You are redeemed] by the precious blood of Christ, as of a lamb without spot or blemish" (I Peter 1, 19). "For these things were done that the Scripture might be fulfilled: You shall not break a bone of him" (John 19, 36). "Behold a Lamb standing as it were slain" (Apoc. 5, 6; read the whole chapter).

The mystical or typical sense is usually subdivided into three kinds or varieties: the allegorical, the tropological, and the anagogical. They correspond to the three theological virtues of faith, hope, and charity.

This clean-cut distinction was not always observed by the early Fathers nor by some later writers.

To avoid confusion, it is well to remember that, in general rhetoric, *allegory* is a " continued metaphor," a variety of the improper literal or metaphorical sense, while among scripturists it is sometimes a variety of the mystical and sometimes a variety of the accommodated sense,— a very ambiguous and bothersome word.

Besides the literal sense, we should admit in some, but not in all, parts of the Old Testament a prophetico-allegorical typical sense, referring to Christ and to His Church, in the distant Messianic period.

This proposition is evident from the testimony of the New Testament writers and from the constant tradition of both Jews and Christians.

Some parts of the Old Testament, especially the Aaronic ritual, are full of instances of the typical sense, full of remarkable types of Christ and His Church, full of events, things, institutions, and persons that foreshadow the principal events of the life of Christ and the glory of His Church.

Instances are: Adam; Noah; the Ark and those saved in it; Melchisedech; Abraham, Sarah, and Isaac; Hagar and Ishmael; David, Solomon, Jonah, and many others, especially the sacrifice of Isaac and the Paschal Lamb.

The interpreter should not be too intent on finding the mystical sense everywhere in Scripture, but should admit it only where the Scriptures or the Church have admitted it, or where the evidence of its presence is clear and convincing; that is, where it is the manifest intention of the author to foreshadow certain things, events, or persons by other things, events or persons; neither should the student attach too much importance to the typical sense for proving doctrines of faith and morals, unless he can prove, with theological certainty, that this sense exists in a given passage and that it possesses decisive argumentative value

## C) *The Accommodated Sense*

There are only two kinds of " sense " in Scripture, the literal and the typical, both of which are intended by the author and both of which we have already defined.

However, much has been written about a *third* kind, called the esthetical or accommodated sense. All writers however acknowledge that to this sense there is not the slightest reference in any passage of Sacred Scripture, whether taken in its literal or in its typical sense. It may be thus *defined:* The *accommodated sense* is a sense which the Sacred Text does not contain and does not express either by words or by things, either in any literal or in any typical sense; but which, on account of some resemblance or analogy with the real sense of the passage, is fixed upon the text by the interpreter, who thus adapts or accommodates to one thing, event, institution or person what the Sacred Writer intended to say about another thing, event, institution or person.

Thus the accommodated sense is not the sense of the Sacred Text, nor of the Inspired Writer. It is a sense which the interpreter puts into the text *(" sensum infert, non effert "),* on account of some resemblance with the real sense of the passage; or, which, in the absence of any such resemblance, he foists upon the text.

The writers of the New Testament, the Fathers of the Church, especially in their homilies, and the Church herself in her liturgy, sometimes quote Scripture in an esthetical or accommodated sense. It is, therefore, allowable and even laudable to do so, provided always the accommodated sense is neither too low, nor too trivial, nor too far-fetched, nor too long spun out, nor too remote from, nor opposed to, nor in any way exclusive of, the true sense of the passage of Scripture, and provided also it is never given out as if it were the true sense, or one of the true senses, of the Sacred Writer and, still less, to the exclusion of the true sense.

## PART II

## HOW TO DISCOVER THE SENSE OF SCRIPTURE

# PART II

# HOW TO DISCOVER THE SENSE OF SCRIPTURE

Sacred Scripture is at the same time (a) a human, (b) a divine, and (c) an ecclesiastical document.

a) Scripture is a *human* document, because it was written by men, for men, in the language of men, and in accordance with the laws of human grammar, rhetoric, and logic, and all this, so that it might be understood by men.

b) Scripture is also a *divine* document, because it was written under the special divine influence, called inspiration, and, accordingly, has God for its principal Author.

c) Scripture (the New Testament) is also called an *ecclesiastical* document, because it was written by members of the teaching corps of the Church (John, Paul, Luke, etc.) while engaged in propagating the faith, and because God appointed the Church to be its official guardian and authentic interpreter in all doctrinal matters, and gave her, as such, the right to impose such interpretations on all her members.

Accordingly, we have, in general, two kinds of principles for interpreting Sacred Scripture; the first is called the *rational,* and the second is called the *dogmatic.*

1. The *rational* principles of Biblical Hermeneutics, as the word rational implies, are based on reason and, therefore, are common to all men, as far as they are men, as far as they are rational beings, as far as they are logical creatures.

Thus, the rational principles of Hermeneutics are, more or less, applicable to Scripture, because Scripture, as said above, is also a human document, a human literary production.

2. The *dogmatic* principles of Biblical Hermeneutics are based on *revelation* and are sub-divided into two kinds: (a) the Christian, and (b) the Catholic.

a) The *Christian* principles of Biblical Hermeneutics are common to all those Christians, Catholic and Protestant alike, who admit the plenary and real inspiration of S. Scripture and its consequent plenary infallibility.

b) The *Catholic* principles of Hermeneutics are peculiar to all those who believe, not only in the plenary inspiration and consequent infallibility of Scripture, but also in the infallibility of the *Church*, as the authentic interpreter of the doctrinal parts of Scripture.[1]

As far as it is *human*, Scripture should be interpreted, more or less, according to the same general principles that are followed in the explanation of other human documents.

As far as it is *divine*, and consequently infallible,

[1] Ranolder was the first to give due prominence to this distinction between the rational, the Christian, and the Catholic principles of Hermeneutics. It is expressed even in the title to his book. His example has been imitated by Dixon, Ubaldi, and many others. In discussing this subject we follow their example in general and sometimes even in detail.

Scripture should be interpreted in such a way as not to admit any error or falsehood in the words of the inspired writers.

As far as it is an *ecclesiastical* literary production, Scripture, in its doctrinal parts, should be interpreted according to " the sense of the Church, the unanimous consent of the Fathers, and the analogy of Catholic Faith."

It is necessary to remember that the *Christian* principle of interpretation, which is founded on the infallibility of Sacred Scripture, is merely *negative* in scope and character; whereas

The *Catholic* principle of interpretation, which is founded on the infallibility of the Church, is both *negative* and *positive*.

The Christian principle tells us how Scripture should *not* be interpreted.

The Catholic principle tells us both how Scripture should *not* be interpreted, and also how it *should be* interpreted.

The Christian principle is opposed to Rationalism.

The Catholic principle is opposed to both Rationalism and Protestantism. Then, in order to discover the sense of Sacred Scripture, we have, all told, five systems of hermeneutics. They are, 1) The Rational, 2) the Christian, 3) the Catholic, 4) the Protestant and 5) the Rationalistic. The three first are all true and are to be retained; the last two are entirely false and to be rejected. We discuss them in order.

# CHAPTER I

# THE RATIONAL PRINCIPLES OF HERMENEUTICS

# CHAPTER I

# THE RATIONAL PRINCIPLES OF HERMENEUTICS

*The Rational Principles of Biblical Interpretation*

As said above, these are based on reason, are common to all who have the use of reason, and are applicable also to Sacred Scripture.

The *first* thing to consider is the *usage* of the language spoken by the people at the time when the writer lived and wrote. The language of his people and of his time and place is independent of the writer and is *objective* and *national*.

The *second* thing to consider is the permanent environment, the civil, political and religious circumstances in which the author lived and wrote, and which must have influenced him in the production of his book. This element is extrinsic to, and independent of, the writer, and is *objective* and *historical*.

The *third* thing to consider is the influence which the writer exercised on the language of his people, time and place, slightly modifying the meaning of words and phrases, so as to make them subservient to his purpose. This element is dependent on the writer and is *subjective* and *personal*.

The first of these is *philological*, the second is *historical*, and the third is *logical*.

The *philological* criteria may all be reduced to what is commonly called the "*usus loquendi*" and this may be considered either (1) in general, or (2) as found in the Hebrew and Greek originals, or (3) in the Latin Vulgate translation, or (4) in Biblical figurative language.

But as some of these branches of Biblical Hermeneutics are so extensive and so minutely detailed and complicated, and as they can be treated to greater advantage in the class-room under the direction of the professor, we say no more about them. We mention them here just to show their place in the course.

Yet we shall explain very briefly the nature of the Biblical *usus loquendi* in general and some peculiarities of Biblical figurative language and the principal rules for interpreting it.

## *The Biblical Usus Loquendi*

The *usus loquendi*, which may be either national or personal, is the constant and uniform manner in which a writer or a people are accustomed to express their thoughts in writing at any given time.

This uniformity mentioned in the definition, is not absolute. All languages, including the Semitic, are subject to change. The language of a people, and still more the language of an individual, will change according to the various circumstances of time and place, of religion and education, of form of government, whether civil or ecclesiastical, of laws and customs, of manners and occupation, and still more, according to the individuality of the writer and the vicissitudes through which he has passed. St. Paul is a good instance.

The most important criteria to follow in this matter are the following:—

(1) The language of a writer is to be understood according to the national *usus loquendi* at the time he wrote and also according to his personal *usus loquendi*, unless grave reasons are alleged to the contrary.

(2) Any interpretation that is opposed to the *usus loquendi*, without sufficiently grave reasons to the contrary, should be rejected as false.

(3) Any interpretation that is suggested by the *usus loquendi* and that is not counterbalanced by weighty considerations to the contrary, should be admitted as true.

*Figurative Language*

The language of the Bible, even in a translation, is *extremely figurative,* abounding in tropes, metaphors, and similitudes without number. Especially the poetical books of the Old Testament are remarkable for the superabundance of their figurative language, for the boldness of their hyperboles, for the exuberance of their metaphors, for the frequency of their tropes, for the wild extravagance of their imagery, and for the vigor, strangeness, redundancy, and profusion of vocabulary and rhetoric poured out on topics of relatively little importance.

A few rules for the right understanding of such language may prove serviceable:

a) The words of Scripture are to be taken in their

obvious, ordinary, literal sense, unless it is manifest that they are to be taken figuratively.

The reason is clear. Literal language is the rule; figurative language is the exception. The rule should be taken for granted, the exception should be proved.

b) The words of Scripture are to be taken in their obvious, ordinary, literal sense, whenever it is the manifest intention of the Sacred Writer to relate historical *facts* or to teach *doctrines*.

c) The words of Scripture are to be taken figuratively, whenever the author clearly implies as much, or when the nature of the case demands it.

## Logical Criteria of Interpretation

Each writer appropriates as much of the national language as he can or will, and manipulates it to suit his purpose, restricting, extending, or otherwise modifying the meaning of certain words according to his needs, or literary tastes, or special occupation, or individual character.

Now, to determine the meaning of certain words, when their precise and exceptional shade of meaning depends, not so much on national, as on personal usage, we have certain indirect criteria of a logical nature, such as context, parallelism, subject matter, scope of the writer, occasion of the writing, any one of which may be of great assistance in determining the meaning of words and phrases and sentences.

## 1. The Context

The context is the connection between what precedes and what follows a given passage or text in the same discourse.

The word context literally means "*woven together*" and is used to indicate the web of a written discourse.

If the connection is between the subject and the predicate, or between the premises and the conclusion, or between the parts and the whole, or between the cause and the effect, or between the genus and the species, the context is called logical.

If, however, the parts are connected by an association of *ideas*, the context is merely psychological.

If the parts are connected in the *order of time*, the context is chronological or historical.

The following rules need no explanation:

(1) Any interpretation that is contrary to the context is false.

(2) Any interpretation which alone agrees with the context may be admitted as true.

(3) If many interpretations suit a passage, that interpretation which best suits the context should be preferred.

The reader will remark that here, as in many other things, the criterion works better negatively than positively.

If the *usus loquendi* does not suffice, the context may be of great assistance in determining the precise signification of ambiguous words and phrases.

A due consideration of the context may show that

the meaning is sometimes to be restricted, or extended, or slightly modified from the usual signification of the words; it will also show whether words are to be taken in their absolute or in their relative sense; also whether words are to be taken in their obvious, ordinary, literal signification, or in a figurative or transferred sense. It may also show what is the precise meaning of the metaphor.

## 2 The Biblical Parallelism

A Biblical parallelism is a resemblance existing between the various parts of the same writing, or between the different writings of the same author.

It is well to remember that, since God is the Author of all Scripture, Biblical parallelisms may exist between any books of the Bible.

The usual division of parallelism is into verbal and real: *verbal*, where the same word or phrase occurs; *real*, where the same thought is expressed, or where the same subject matter is discussed. Real parallelisms are sub-divided into doctrinal and historical: *doctrinal*, where the same truth is inculcated; *historical*, where the same event or series of events is recorded.

When neither the *usus loquendi* nor the context can decide the signification of words, a careful examination of parallel passages may be of great help. It often happens that what is obscure or ambiguous in one passage is explained by reference to a parallel passage, where everything is clear and explicit. Due consideration of parallel passages may also restrict or extend or otherwise modify the meaning of words, or show whether they are to be taken literally or metaphorically and what is the precise meaning of the metaphor.

### 3. *The Subject Matter*

The subject matter is that of which the author treats; it is the topic which he handles; it is the theme which he discusses. It may be the theme either of the *whole* book or of only a *part* of the book. Rules to be observed·

(1) Any interpretation that is opposed to the subject matter is to be rejected as false

(2) Any interpretation that is the only one to agree with the subject matter may be admitted as true.

(3) If many interpretations agree with a passage, that interpretation which best suits the subject matter should be preferred to the others.

A due consideration of the subject matter will explain ambiguous or obscure words or phrases, it will restrict or extend or modify the signification of words; it will show whether words are to be taken in their literal or in their figurative sense and also whether the words are to be taken absolutely or relatively, and what is the precise meaning of its metaphor. See I Cor. 9, 20; Matt. 19, 24; Matt. 12, 22; Heb. 6, 4; Matt. 10, 22; John 3, 32; Matt. 6, 34; 5, 34.

### 4. *The Scope of the Writer*

The scope of the writer is the end, or aim, or purpose for which he writes his book.

It is sometimes necessary to distinguish the *special*

purpose of a part of the book from the *general* purpose of the whole book. Rules to be observed:

(1) Any interpretation that is clearly opposed to the scope of the writer is to be rejected as false.

(2) Any interpretation which alone agrees with the scope of the writer may be retained as true.

(3) If many interpretations agree with the scope of the writer, that interpretation which best of all agrees with his purpose should be preferred to the others.

Due consideration for the scope of the writer will enable the interpreter to explain obscure and ambiguous words or phrases; to decide whether words are to be understood absolutely or relatively, in a universal or in a restricted sense, in a literal or in a figurative sense and also to give the precise meaning of the figure. (See Matt. 16, 18–19; 25, 13.)

## 5. *The Occasion of Writing*

The occasion of writing is some *external circumstance* which moved the author to write.

The occasion of writing is much like the scope of the writer and sometimes can hardly be distinguished from it.

The usefulness and necessity of this criterion to the interpreter of Scripture are about the same as those of the scope of the writer and need not be repeated.

# CHAPTER II

# CHRISTIAN PRINCIPLES OF HERMENEUTICS

## CHAPTER II

## CHRISTIAN PRINCIPLES OF HERMENEUTICS

The rational principles of Hermeneutics are based on reason and are therefore common to all men as far as they are men, that is, rational, logical beings. These principles are applicable here, because Scripture is a human document. But Scripture is also a divine document, because it is inspired by the Holy Ghost; and it is also a canonical document, because it is declared divine by a solemn judgment of the Church, and the Church is both the official guardian and the infallible interpreter of Holy Scripture.

From this it follows that there are two Christian criteria or principles of Hermeneutics:

1. The infallibility of *Scripture,* which directly follows from its inspiration, and

2. The authentic or infallible judgment of the *Church,* which follows from her infallibility.

These are called the dogmatic principles of interpretation.

Now, since these principles are admitted, or at least should be admitted logically, by all Christians, they are called Christian principles; or, rather, the first principle is Christian, and the second, being peculiar to Catholics, is called the Catholic principle.

The Rationalists reject both and insist exclusively on the rational principles of Hermeneutics.

Against the Rationalists we shall first establish the Christian criteria;

Against Protestants we shall later establish the Catholic criteria.

*First Proposition*

*The Books of Scripture are to be interpreted in such a way as to admit no error in the words of the inspired writers.*

We say, "no error"; that is, not only no error against faith or morals, as in dogmatic passages, but also no error in any other matter; for instance, in historical or scientific passages, or in things of even lesser importance.

We add, "in the words of the inspired writers" there is no error. For it is not repugnant to the inspiration of Scripture that it should contain false statements in *quotations* made by men who were not inspired, and quoted into Scripture by the inspired writers, but without approval.

Our proposition is proved, (1) by the very notion of inspiration. Inspiration is an act of such a kind that it makes God the author, the principal author, of Sacred Scripture.

From this it follows that hermeneutical truth is identical with objective truth. Then, whenever we find the real meaning of a passage, *i. e.*, the meaning intended by the Sacred Writer, that meaning is *in se* and objectively true. And any meaning that is *in se* false, can not be the meaning intended by the Sacred Writer, — can not be hermeneutically true.

The proposition is proved also (2) by the practice of the Church and the Fathers. In defending any passage of Scripture against pagans and heretics, the Fathers could never be induced to admit even the slightest error in the sacred text; and, no matter how embarrassing the difficulties might be, they would rather acknowledge their own ignorance than admit that Scripture had erred. It is well to know that the Fathers acted thus, not only in regard to doctrinal passages of Scripture, but also in historical and scientific passages and things of lesser moment. This is all the more remarkable, as we know that they were ready to reject statements made by other authors, no matter how great their authority, so long as they were not inspired. This shows that the Fathers considered the Scriptures inspired and infallible in every part.

Since there are many things in Sacred Scripture which *seem* to be false, but yet are *true,* we will examine some of the many ways of explaining them away. For the sake of clearness, we will consider in order (1) doctrinal and (2) historical passages.

1. As to *doctrinal* passages, the rule is this: If the sense of Scripture is clear and altogether certain, and if some philosophical principle or scientific conclusion, which seems to clash with it, is obscure and uncertain, reason requires that the latter should be subordinated to the former and should be so understood as to agree or, rather, as not to disagree with Scripture.

In other words, the *obscure* should be interpreted in

the light of the *clear*. By so doing, no injury is done to either philosophy or science. Truth can not contradict truth; science can not contradict Revelation. On the contrary, science has been much assisted by Revelation, especially those sciences that are still in their infancy. Scientists frequently enunciate principles too broadly and draw sweeping and universal conclusions from a limited number of facts. Sometimes, too, their ideas are not accurately defined and need revision; sometimes their conclusions are not universally true, but admit some exception, restriction, or limitation, and often, when not already exploded by other scientists, they are corrected by Revelation, of which we have so many instances.

2. On the other hand, if some philosophical principle or some scientific conclusion is thoroughly established, and if some passage of Scripture, which seems to clash with it, is obscure and ambiguous, then reason requires that the passage of Scripture should be interpreted so as to agree or, rather, so as not to disagree, with science or philosophy.

In other words, the *obscure* should be interpreted in the light of the *clear*. By so doing, no injury is done to Sacred Scripture Truth can not contradict truth; so Scripture, when properly understood, can not contradict the well established conclusions of philosophy or of science. On the contrary, the interpretation of Scripture has often been assisted by science, especially where there is question of interpreting the natural sciences, which are often expressed in Scripture in a broad and popular style and not with scientific accuracy.

Yet, whenever there is opposition between them, they should be reconciled. This may be done in two ways:

a) By showing that, when Sacred Scripture is taken in its hermeneutical sense, there is really no opposition to science; or

b) By showing that the passage of Sacred Scripture is not to be taken in its strict or rigorous sense, but in a broad and relative sense. In questions especially belonging to the natural sciences, such as physics, etc., Scripture is often to be understood as the Sacred Writer himself meant it to be understood, namely, in a broad and popular sense.

This is the theory advanced by such great luminaries as St. Augustine, St. Thomas, and Leo XIII. The words of St. Augustine apropos of this subject, are found toward the close of his first book on "The Literal Interpretation of Genesis." Centuries later, St. Thomas applied the wise counsel of Augustine to the circumstances of his own times. It is equally applicable in our own day. Writing about the work of the Second Day, St. Thomas says that "In questions of this sort there are two things to be observed: First, that the truth of Scripture should be inviolably maintained; second, since many parts of Scripture admit of many different interpretations, we must not cling to any one particular exposition with such pertinacity that, if what we supposed to be the teaching of Scripture should afterwards turn out to be clearly false, we should nevertheless still presume to put it forward; lest, thereby, we should expose the Inspired Word of God to the derision of unbelievers, and shut them out from the way of salvation." *(Summa Theologica,* Ia, qu. 68, Art. 1.)

As to *historical passages:* if anything in Scripture seems to be opposed to what we know from other sources, we should seriously attempt to reconcile the opposing statements. This is often easy. It sometimes happens that circumstances mentioned by one writer are supplied by another. Also when the difference of times, and the order of facts, and the diversity of proper names of persons and places, mentioned by sacred and by profane writers, are considered carefully in a practical and sympathetic spirit, the difficulties often vanish. Of this we have many instances, which, for the sake of brevity, we omit.

But, if no reconciliation seems possible, we must, as a rule, either *suspend judgment* or throw the profane writer overboard And this may very properly be done. Often enough, when we can not follow both, we are *compelled* to abandon one profane writer to follow another profane writer. Then, why may we not abandon a profane writer to follow a sacred writer? Profane writers often contradict one another and sometimes one contradicts himself Then why may we not contradict each of them and even both of them? All the more so, as the inspired writer treats, generally speaking, not of the affairs of distant nations, but of his own people, country, and time, in which he may have been an eye-witness or even an agent. Herodotus and several other classical writers lived thousands of miles and hundreds of years distant from many of the events which they describe, and thus fell into error.

## Second Proposition

*Sacred Scripture is to be interpreted in such a way that no contradiction shall ever be admitted between the statements of inspired writers.*

A contradiction is an affirmation and a negation of the same quality or attribute about the same thing and under the same respect. *("Contradictio est affirmatio et negatio eiusdem de eodem sub eodem.")* In Greek it is called an antilogy.

A contradiction is *real*, if the opposing statements can in no way be reconciled. It is *apparent*, if they can in some way be reconciled. Now, since God is the one primary Author of all Scripture, to admit that one Biblical writer can contradict another Biblical writer, would be to admit that God can contradict Himself,— which is impossible.

The first proof of our proposition is derived from the preceding proposition. For where there can be *no real error*, there can be *no real contradiction*, for we know from logic that, of two contradictory statements, one must be false. But there is no falsity in Scripture.

The second proof for our proposition is derived from the practice of the Church and of the Fathers. What we said about them in the preceding thesis will apply here and need not be repeated.

How are we to explain apparent contradictions?

Their causes are either (1) general or (2) special.

The general causes can be reduced to three, which St. Augustine explains in his famous trilemma.

(1) The first cause of apparent contradictions in

Scripture may be *defective transcription,*— the result of accident or the fault of some subsequent scribe. In such a case, we must get the correct original reading of the text in question.

(2) The second cause of apparent contradictions in Scripture may be *faulty translation.* In such a case, we should get a better translation or should work on the original text.

(3) The third cause of apparent contradictions in Scripture may be our own *faulty conception* or our *ignorance.* This cause may sometimes be removed by study; but sometimes it remains, because we have not the necessary data to judge by.

The special causes are too numerous to be mentioned.

*Apparent* contradictions may be found (1) in historical, (2) in dogmatic passages.

(1) In historical passages, apparent contradictions are frequently caused by *errors of transcription* in numbers (for instance, I Kings 13, 1), or by a *different manner of writing.* Some write profusely and give precise details, dates and figures, whereas others relate all such things briefly, *in globo,* in round numbers (" *circa, circiter* "). Precision is not always aimed at. For the sake of brevity it is often undesirable. Of this we have many instances. Compare, *e.g.,* Gen. 15, 15 with Ex. 12, 40. According to the first, Israel remained 400 years in Egypt; according to the second, 430 years.

Also, apparent contradictions are frequently caused by the *different persons speaking or writing.* Compare I Kings 31, 4 with II Kings 1, 10.

(2) In doctrinal passages, apparent contradictions often depend on *the double meaning of words.* Compare Gen. 22, 1, where it is said that God "tempted Abraham," with James 1, 13, where it is said that " God tempts no man." In the first case, " to tempt " means to try; in the second case, it means to endeavor to lead into sin.

Apparent contradictions often depend on the different times and places and other circumstances in which things were done; of which we have innumerable instances.

# CHAPTER III

# CATHOLIC PRINCIPLES OF HERMENEUTICS

# CHAPTER III

## CATHOLIC PRINCIPLES OF HERMENEUTICS

The *Christian principle of interpretation,* which we have just considered, is common to all those who believe in the plenary and real inspiration and in the consequent plenary *infallibility of Sacred Scripture.* This principle is good as far as it goes, but it does not' go far enough.

The *Catholic principle of interpretation,* which we are now to consider, is common to all those who believe also in the *infallibility of the Church,* not only in defining faith and morals in general, as found in divine tradition, but also and especially in defining the doctrines of faith and morals as contained in Sacred Scripture.

It is necessary to remember, as already stated, that the Christian principle of interpretation, which is founded on the infallibility of Sacred Scripture, is *merely negative* in scope and character, but that the Catholic principle of interpretation, which is founded on the infallibility of the Church, is *both negative* and *positive.*

The Christian principle tells us how Scripture should *not* be interpreted.

The Catholic principle tells us both how Scripture

should *not* be interpreted, and also how it *should* be interpreted.

The Christian principle is opposed to Rationalism

The Catholic principle is opposed both to Rationalism and to Protestantism.

To avoid confusion in this important matter, it is necessary to explain certain fundamental notions of Catholic theology in regard to the authority of the Church as interpreter of Sacred Scripture.

The theologian will remember that the Church is accustomed to interpret Scripture in two ways. The first way is special and direct; the second way is general and indirect.

1. According to the *first or direct way*, the Church, either (a) by an express definition of Pope or ecumenical council, solemnly defines, or, (b) by the unanimous consent of the Fathers, given in a more informal manner, she declares the meaning of some definite, special doctrinal passage of Sacred Scripture.

2. According to *the second or indirect way*, the Church does not define, nay does not even mention any definite passage of Scripture, but declares her revealed doctrines absolutely; absolutely, that is to say, without perhaps even the remotest reference to, or mention of, any passage of Sacred Scripture. In other words, she defines the doctrine received from divine tradition and contained in the general deposit of faith, just as she would define it, even if Scripture had never been written or did not exist.

Then, if the special doctrine thus defined by the Church, happens to be found also in Scripture, the

CATHOLIC PRINCIPLES 49

clear exposition of that doctrine by the Church will necessarily throw, and cannot but throw, much light on those passages of Scripture in which the same doctrine is contained. This is called the analogy of Catholic faith. We shall speak, first, of the direct and, secondly, of the indirect method, of interpreting Sacred Scripture.

*The Direct or Special Method of Interpreting Sacred Scripture*

The decree "*Insuper*" of the Council of Trent was promulgated for the purpose of correcting various abuses regarding the editing and use of Sacred Scripture, including some false methods of interpretation. This decree is, therefore, here in order and reads as follows:

" Moreover, in order to restrain turbulent spirits, the Council declares that no one, relying on his own skill and distorting the sense of Scripture to suit himself, in matters of faith and morals, belonging to the building up of Christian doctrine, shall presume to interpret Sacred Scripture contrary to the sense which Holy Mother Church — to whom it belongs to judge of the true sense and interpretation of Holy Scripture — both held and continues to hold; nor [shall any one dare to interpret] Sacred Scripture contrary to the unanimous consent of the Fathers." [1]

[1] "*Praeterea ad coercenda petulantia ingenia, decernit [Sancta Synodus] ut nemo, suae prudentiae innixus, in rebus fidei et morum, ad aedificationem doctrinae Christianae pertinentium, Sacram Scripturam ad suos sensus contorquens, contra eum (1) sensum quem tenuit et tenet Sancta Mater Ecclesia, cuius est iudicare de vero sensu et interpretatione Scripturarum*

## The Rules Laid Down by Trent

A very superficial examination of this decree will suffice to show that in it there is question of two criteria of Hermeneutics, the *sense of the Church* and the *unanimous consent of the Fathers*. These two criteria lead naturally to the formation of the following two rules or propositions:

(1) In interpreting the doctrinal passages of Scripture, we must follow the *sense* of the Church.

(2) In interpreting the doctrinal passages of Scripture, we must follow the *unanimous consent* of the Fathers.

Before attempting to establish these rules, we should consider, in general, what was the mind of the Council in this decree and should ask ourselves, (1) Why these two rules are treated separately by the Council? (2) What is their object? (3) What is their value? and (4) What is their character?

1. Since, according to the principles of sound theology, the consent of the Fathers has authority in such matters only as far as it represents the sense of the Church and is identified with it, we ask, why are the "sense of the Church" and the "unanimous consent of the Fathers" treated *separately* in this decree?

We answer that the Church is accustomed to declare her mind on dogmatic questions (among which are comprised her interpretations of doctrinal passages of Scripture) in either of these two ways:

<small>Sanctarum, aut etiam contra (2) unanimem consensum Patrum, ipsam Scripturam Sacram interpretari audeat" (Sess IV, Decree on the Editing and Use of the Sacred Books.)</small>

## CATHOLIC PRINCIPLES

(a) The Church sometimes, by a *formal definition* of either pope or ecumenical council, declares the meaning of some doctrinal passage of Scripture.

(b) The Church sometimes promulgates no special decree, no formal definition, but, *by her daily and ordinary teaching,* shows what she holds in regard to the sense of some doctrinal passage of Scripture.

Now, in the decree "*Insuper*" the "sense of the Church" is identical with the first or *formal* way of teaching, and the "unanimous consent of the Fathers" is identical with the second or *informal* way. And though these two ways are the same radically and in *substance,* yet they are practically distinct in *form* and present themselves to us as proximately constituting two distinct norms or rules of interpretation.

Besides, for the first, we must go to the decrees of popes and councils; for the second, we must apply to the much more voluminous writings of the Fathers.

2. The object of these two rules is clearly stated in these words of the Council: "In things of faith and morals pertaining to the building up of Christian doctrine." Hence, as far as demanded by *this* decree, these rules need to be observed only in those parts of Scripture which treat of *faith* and *morals* and are generally called "dogmatic passages."

Therefore, these rules need not be observed in those parts of Scripture which treat of *other things,* such as history, biography, geography, geology, astronomy and the natural sciences generally.

The Church has never claimed and has never exercised any direct and positive authority in interpreting the non-doctrinal portions of Holy Writ, but only an *indirect* and *negative* authority, which we shall explain later.

Though Sacred Scripture is inspired in all its parts, and consequently is infallibly true in all its parts, still the Church does not claim to be infallible in interpreting *all*, but only the *doctrinal*, parts of S. Scripture, that being sufficient for the purpose for which she was instituted,— to save souls.

3. On account of the final clause, which contains the *sanction*, some writers maintained that this decree is transient and temporary in character and purpose, and that it has little or no binding force. They held that the decree was published merely on account of the peculiar circumstances of the times, which were turbulent and almost anarchical; also that, if the circumstances ever again became normal, this legislation would cease to exist almost, if not quite, automatically; also that the circumstances had already so much changed for the better that the law no longer existed, or, at least, that it does not bind in conscience *(in foro interno)*, but only *in foro externo;* also that, if it does bind at all *in foro interno*, it does not bind *sub gravi*, but only *sub levi;* also that it does not oblige in conscience, unless one is caught violating it and then it obliges one only to take the consequences and to submit to the punishment.

But that this decree, especially in the part which regards the explanation of *doctrinal* passages, is not merely a penal law, binding *in foro externo* only, but that it is a precept obliging in conscience *(in foro in-*

## CATHOLIC PRINCIPLES

*'terno)* and under pain of grievous sin, and that it is a permanent legislation, is as manifest as it well can be:

1. From the solemn words of the Council, which " declares that no one shall dare to interpret," etc., and

2. From the grave penalties to be inflicted upon those who violate the law. " They who disobey shall be punished, etc.," according to the prescriptions of Canon Law; and

3. From the " Adnotationes " of the "Commissio Theologica" of the Vatican Council, which shows that all the above statements are thoroughly false.

That part of the decree *" Insuper "* which refers to the interpretation of dogmatic parts of Scripture, can easily be reduced to Catholic doctrinal principles and is, by its very nature or subject-matter, capable of being defined as an article of faith. In fact, the doctrinal principle is clearly enunciated in the decree itself, in just so many words, where it says: " It belongs to the Church to judge of the true sense and interpretation of Scripture." For this and other reasons, some very distinguished Catholic theologians have maintained that this decree or, at least, this part of the decree, is dogmatic, not only in substance, but also in form. But their number seems to be rapidly diminishing. In the chapter on the Latin Vulgate (Vol. I) we have proved to our own satisfaction that this decree *" Insuper,"* as promulgated by the Council of Trent, though dogmatic in a part of its *substance,* is only disciplinary in *form.*

Many of our most conservative and cautious Scripturists openly acknowledge that the Council of Trent does not propose this or any other part of this decree in the form of a dogmatic definition, but merely as a practical precept or rule for the guidance of clergy and people. To make a part of it dogmatic was reserved to the Council of the Vatican.

That this decree of Trent is only disciplinary in form, is evident from the whole *tenor* and *context*, and also from the peculiar sanction attached to it; for the sanction is not an anathema against those who *deny*, as is usually the case in dogmatic utterances, but is merely a canonical punishment to be inflicted by the Ordinary of the diocese on those who *disobey*.

We say, the decree "*Insuper,*" as promulgated by the Council of *Trent,* is only disciplinary in form; at the same time, it is very necessary to the Catholic student to know that that precise part (a short but important part) of the decree which mentions the "sense of the Church" in explaining doctrinal passages of Scripture, by the way it is inserted into the "Constitutio dogmatica" of the Council of the *Vatican,* has been made an article of faith or a dogma of the Catholic Church and, as such, it is now immutable and irreformable for time and eternity.

All the rest of the decree, including even the part referring to "the unanimous consent of the Fathers," the wording of which was not changed by the Council, very probably remains merely disciplinary in form, as it was when promulgated by the Council of Trent.

The Decree reads: "Forasmuch as the wholesome decree of the Sacred Council of Trent concerning the interpretation of Divine Scripture . . . has been perversely explained by divers persons, We, while renewing the said decree, declare that this is its meaning: that, in matters of faith and morals pertaining to the building up of Christian doctrine, that is to be held as the true sense of Sacred Scripture which Holy Mother Church has held and continues to hold, to whom it belongs to judge of the true sense and interpretation of Holy Scripture; and, therefore, no one is allowed to interpret the said Scripture against this sense or even against the unanimous consent of the Fathers." [1]

### Third Proposition

*In explaining passages of Scripture that pertain to faith and morals, the Catholic interpreter should follow " the sense which the Church has held and still holds."*

The meaning of this proposition is as clear and categorical as need be. The proofs for it are equally clear and conclusive.

The fundamental argument for this proposition is expressly indicated by the Council itself in these words of the decree " *Insuper* ": " It belongs to the Church to judge of the true sense and interpretation of Sacred Scripture." Since this statement is, of course, true, we argue from it thus:

[1] "*Nos idem decretem [Tridentinum] renovantes, hanc illius [decreti] mentem esse declaramus, ut in rebus fidei et morum, ad aedificationem doctrinae Christianae pertinentium, is PRO VERO SENSU Sacrae Scripturae habendus sit, quem tenuit et tenet Sancta Mater Ecclesia, cuius est iudicare de VERO SENSU et INTERPRETATIONE Sacrarum Scripturarum, atque ideo nemini licere contra hunc sensum, aut etiam contra unanimem consensum Sanctorum PATRUM ipsam Scripturam interpretari*" (Sessio III, "*De Fide Catholica,*" C. II, *De Revelatione.*)

*Major:* In explaining doctrinal passages of Scripture, the Catholic interpreter should follow the sense of the one whose right and duty it is to judge of the true sense and interpretation of Sacred Scripture.

*Minor:* But, according to the words of the decree, above quoted, it is the right and the duty of the *Church* to judge of the true sense and interpretation of Sacred Scripture.

*Conclusion:* Therefore, in explaining passages of Scripture which pertain to faith and morals, the Catholic interpreter should follow the sense which the Church has held and still holds.

The major of this syllogism is evident. The minor is proved (1) by direct, and (2) by indirect arguments.

1. By *direct arguments.*—An interpretation is called authentic, if it comes from the author of the law. But an interpretation may come from the author of the law in either of two ways: (a) *Immediately,* when the legislator himself personally explains the meaning of the law; (b) *mediately,* when the interpretation is given by some one who officially represents the legislator and acts in his name and by his authority.

We say that the interpretations given by the Church to dogmatic passages of Scripture are always authentic, sometimes immediately, sometimes mediately, and sometimes in both ways together.

a) The doctrinal interpretations given to Scripture by the Church are always authentic, at least *mediately.*

In fundamental theology we are taught that the Church is always infallible in faith and morals. This is especially true when there is question of the sense of

## CATHOLIC PRINCIPLES

the doctrinal parts of Scripture; for nothing can belong more to the teaching office of the Church than the exposition of the word of God. We should realize that Sacred Scripture not only belongs to the deposit of faith, but that it is one of the two *channels* through which many revealed doctrines reach us. Therefore, the Church is infallible in defining the doctrinal contents of Scripture

The proposition is further proved by the fact that the Church, *antecedently* to, and *independently* of, Scripture, possesses the meaning of the whole body of revealed truth As this is an important fact and a fundamental and very useful theological principle, it deserves special explanation

From the very beginning, in fact from the first Pentecost Sunday, the Church was full-fledged. She was thoroughly equipped for her work; she was in possession of relatively the entire body of revealed truth; she was furnished with a hierarchical order, having authority from Christ to govern and to teach; she had her sacramental system for conferring grace and sanctifying souls; she was engaged in her mission of Christianizing and civilizing the nations throughout, and even beyond, the limits of the Graeco-Roman world and was sending myriads of saints to Heaven; and all this was in full operation for about twenty years before the first book of the New Testament (Thess ? Galat. ?) was written; and for sixty years before the last book of the New Testament (St. John's Gospel) was written. And this because the *Church is older than the Bible.* The Jewish Church or Synagogue existed a thousand years before the last books of the Old Testament were written, and the Christian Church existed and labored with tremendous energy and phenomenal success for sixty years before the New Testament was completed.

Thus, the Church received, through divine tradition, and still possesses, the whole doctrine of Christ. But this whole doctrine, with the explanations of it given by Christ, was never all committed to writing at any time in the New Testament For the Apostles, in their occasional writings, purposely omitted things which, they well knew, had already been taught by some Apostle or Apostolic man to their Christian readers, when the Faith was first preached among them.

To some it may seem strange, but it is still a fact, that the New Testament was originally intended (not for pagans, who could never make anything out of it, but) for Christians, to recall to their minds what they had already learned by oral tradition.

St. Paul and other New Testament writers frequently allude to the more complete antecedent instruction which had been given by some Apostle to their Christian readers. (Coloss. 2, 6–8; I Tim. 6, 20; II Tim. 1, 13; 2, 1–2; 3, 14;)

Therefore, the Church, having the full knowledge of the entire deposit of faith, can, better than any private individual, judge of the real, true sense of particular portions of Scripture, because of the light cast by the whole upon any of the parts.

b) The doctrinal interpretations of the Church are

sometimes authentic *immediately*. The Church still possesses the interpretations given to her by Christ or by the Holy Ghost, through the Apostles, before the death of the last Apostle. We know that Our Lord was accustomed not only to teach New Testament doctrines, but also to explain Old Testament doctrinal passages. For instance, on one occasion, in the Synagogue at Nazareth, He explained the lesson of the day or the text of the Old Testament that had just been read in the service. Also, on the way to Emmaus, on the first Easter Sunday, He explained to the two disciples all that was written about His death and Resurrection in the law of Moses and in the prophets and in the Psalms (Luke 24, 27). Also, during the forty days that he was with them after His Resurrection, He frequently appeared to them and spoke to them of the kingdom of God (Acts 1, 3). This, no doubt, was a continuation of the custom which he had followed during the three years in which He had lived with them on earth.

Again we read that " He opened their mind that they might understand the Scriptures " (Luke 24, 44–46). And the things that He told them, they were *not allowed* to forget, for " the Holy Ghost, whom the Father will send in My name, He will teach you all things, and bring all things to your mind, whatsoever I shall have said to you " (John 14, 26).

Such interpretations the Church, of course, treasured up as a part of the original deposit of faith and, when necessary, she produces them under the direction of the same Holy Ghost, the great Reminder " who brings to their mind all things whatsoever the Lord had said to them."

2. By *indirect argument,* as follows:

*Major.* It is evident that there must necessarily be some authentic interpreter of Sacred Scripture, especially in those parts that are obscure and that pertain to faith and morals.

*Minor.* But if you exclude the Church, there will be no authentic interpreter of Sacred Scripture.

*Conclusion.* Therefore the Church is the authentic interpreter of Sacred Scripture.

The *major* is proved by considering that Scripture, besides being very obscure, is also one of the two parts of the remote rule of faith and morals, that is, it is one of the two channels through which we receive many other revealed truths.

Scripture is also a religious code, in which *grave* laws are imposed and *severe* penalties are inflicted for violating those laws. All this shows that Scripture needs an authentic interpreter, lest mistakes be made in such important matters.

The natural tendency of laws is to restrict liberty, and as restriction of liberty is something odious to human nature, it is as clear as clear can be that no code of laws can long continue to be obeyed, or even to exist, without an authentic interpreter to explain their meaning and to enforce their observance.

Bishop John Milner says: " In supposing Our Savior to have appointed His bare written word for the rule of faith, without any authorized judge to decide the unavoidable controversies growing out of it, you suppose that He has acted differently from what common sense has dictated to all other legislators. For where do we read of a legislator, who, after dictating a code of laws, neglected to appoint a supreme court of appeal, consisting of judges and magistrates, to decide on their meaning and to enforce obedience to their requirements? You know what would be the consequence of having an Act of Parliament or any other similar affair left to the interpretation of the individuals whom it concerns. Fenélon says: "It would be better to live without any laws than to have laws which every man would be left free to explain according to his own opinion and interest.[1]

The *minor* is proved by the absence of any fit interpreter that any one has ever mentioned as a substitute for the Church. To replace the Church, Protestants have tried two different methods of interpreting Scripture: (1) the testimony of the Spirit and (2) private judgment. But further down we shall make it very manifest that neither of these can, by any means, be considered the authentic interpreter of Scripture. Besides, Protestants have never agreed among themselves in the use of these methods.

### Fourth Proposition

*In explaining passages of Scripture that pertain to faith and morals, the Catholic interpreter must follow that sense which the Fathers have given with unanimous consent and settled conviction.*

[1] *End of Controversy,* VIIIth Letter.

*Explanation*

This proposition needs to be explained as well as proved.

By Fathers of the Church we mean, not all ancient ecclesiastical writers, but only those early Christian writers who were remarkable alike for their *antiquity, learning* and *holiness* of life. Their number is great, but not determined. They begin with St. Clement of Rome, in the days of the Apostles, and end with St. Bernard of Clairvaux, in the twelfth century.

1. In our proposition we say that we need to follow the doctrinal interpretations of the Fathers, but only when given with " unanimous consent." Of course, it is not necessary that their consent should be absolutely and mathematically unanimous, else this rule would seldom or never apply. A relative or virtual unanimity is sufficient; but when consent is relatively or virtually unanimous, cannot well be decided in general terms, but must be determined in each concrete case and on the merits of the case.

We may say, however, that we have a moral or relative unanimity whenever the larger and more illustrious number of the Fathers agree in giving an interpretation; also we have a virtual or presumptive unanimity, whenever only a few Fathers give an interpretation, but give it *positively* and *absolutely* as that of the Church, and provided the other Fathers, who flourished at that, or some subsequent time, say nothing to the contrary. In such a case " Silence gives consent."

2. In our proposition we say that this authority of

the Fathers is expressly restricted to things belonging to *faith and morals*. And naturally; for, if the Church herself does not claim infallibility in explaining other than doctrinal passages of Scripture, so neither should the Fathers; for in such matters they simply re-echo the voice of the Church and are identified with it.

This restriction to faith and morals is of very great importance, though often forgotten by some of our Catholic exegetes, who generously pile up quotations from the writings of the Fathers, just as if their word could always settle all sorts of questions,— historical, biographical, geographical, scientific, as well as matters of faith and morals.

We reverence the Fathers for their learning and piety; but these are not the precise reasons why we accept their doctrinal interpretation of Scripture. In things not of faith or morals, we are not obliged to follow the consent of the Fathers, howsoever unanimous. St. Thomas says: "*In his, quae de necessitate fidei non sunt, licuit sanctis diversimode opinari, sicut et nobis.*" (*Comment in Sent.*, II, dist. II, quaest. I, art. 3).

We follow the Fathers, but only when they speak as "*testes traditionis,*"— as witnesses to the tradition of the Church.

We follow the Fathers, when they speak as the oracles or mouth-pieces of the Church, which stands, as it were, behind them and speaks through them. But when they speak as *private* doctors, their interpretations are worth no more than the reasons which they allege in support of them. We must not place too much reliance on the mere conjectures of the Fathers, or on their gropings in the dark, as if these were positive evidence of the tradition of the Church.

3. Again, we need to follow the unanimous consent of the Fathers, but only when it is given, "*with settled conviction*" or with absolute certainty; that is, when they propose an interpretation without doubt or hesitation, or as something fixed and settled, and no longer subject to discussion, but to be accepted independently of all hermeneutical reasons. In such a case, the Fathers show that *it is not because of such hermeneutical reasons* (if any are assigned) that they give the interpretation, but only because *they have received it from the Church.*

## Proof

Our proposition is proved, (1) by a moral, and (2), by a theological argument.

(1) As to the *moral argument,* unless the Fathers, in such cases as we suppose, had received from the Church the interpretations which they give us, it would be morally impossible to explain their agreement.

To understand this, we should remember that we are not now speaking of those passages of Sacred Scripture that are so clear and transparent that agreement is almost necessary; but we are speaking about passages (and there are many of them), the meaning of which is extremely difficult on account of the sublimity or profundity of thought, or on account of the obscurity of the language, or the difficulty of the construction, or because the sense has been distorted by heretics.

From this it is evident that if the sense of such passages were left to each individual interpreter, it would be morally impossible to expect that all the Fathers should agree in giving to them one and the same interpretation.

This is especially true when we reflect how numerous are the Fathers, and how they differ from one another in early training, in education, in local and national prejudices, and in time, place and general culture.

When under such circumstances, we find the Fathers all agreed, we may reasonably infer that they agree, not because they have *all reasoned out* the meaning of the texts independently of one another and in the same way and by the same hermeneutical processes, but because they have *all learned and accepted* the same interpretation from the Church. Under such peculiar circumstances, it is only the voice and the authority of the Church that could produce such Unanimity.

(2) As to the theological argument. If the interpretation of the Fathers, in the circumstances above described, were false, the Church herself would also be guilty of the same error; for, in such a case, it would be impossible to separate the sense of the Church from the unanimous consent of the Fathers. They simply *re-echoed* the voice of the Church, and so, if they erred, she also erred,— which is impossible.

## Objections Refuted

a) It is objected that these rules of the Council of Trent restrict our liberty and are therefore unjust and tyrannical. We reply: Nothing could be more absurd than this accusation. *Intellectual* liberty does not mean that a man may *think* and speak just as he chooses, be it true or false; just as *moral* liberty does not mean that a man may *do* just as he chooses, be it good or bad. Unrestrained freedom is not liberty; it is license; it is anarchy. The head, the heart, and the hand are all subject to God and to law and order, and it is no tyranny to compel them to do their duty. No man has the moral right to reject the truth, but every man should be glad to accept it. The truth is good for its own sake, independently of the effort made to acquire it. So the easier and the sooner a man gets it, the better, provided he gets it.

The light-house, which shows the mariner how to steer his course so as to avoid shipwreck on the rocks, does not restrict his liberty, but is intended for his protection.

b) It is objected that these rules of Trent retard progress. For, as soon as the interpreter is persuaded that nothing more is left for him to do, than to follow in the footsteps of the Fathers, he concludes that nothing more remains to be done.

To this we reply: The rules of Trent in this matter do not regard *all*, but only the *dogmatic* parts of Scripture. In all the rest the exegete is free. Nor do these rules practically concern *all*, but only *some*, even of the dogmatic passages of Scripture. For neither the Church nor the Fathers have ever explained more than a very small portion of the doctrinal passages of Scripture. Then again, in all the rest (not authen-

## CATHOLIC PRINCIPLES

tically explained), the exegete is still free Finally, these rules do not deprive us of the liberty and duty of examining even the official interpretations of the Church or of the Fathers, for the purpose of *elucidating, defending,* and *confirming* them by proper exegetical methods.

### Fifth Proposition

*The decree "Insuper" of Trent, containing the two preceding rules or propositions, is not only negative, but also positive in character and purpose.*

Misled by the negative form in which this part of the decree is expressed, some Catholic writers maintained that this legislation is merely negative,— negative not only in form, but also in sense and substance. They said that the decree is in no way positive, that it gives no positive direction how Scripture *should be* explained, but merely tells us how Scripture *should not be* explained.

About two hundred and fifty years after the Council of Trent, John Jahn, Professor of Scripture at Vienna, was the first to teach that this part of the decree is not positive, but only negative. (Introduction, P. I., § 91.) In this respect his example was followed by Arigler (*Hermen. Bib Gen.*), Lang (*Patrology*) and Moehler *(Symbolik).* They argued that by the words, "sense of the Church," the Council did not mean that particular interpretation which was put by the Church on a special passage of Scripture, but any of the doctrines of the Church in general. Hence, they said, it is not forbidden by this decree to explain doctrinal passages of Scripture contrary to the interpretation which the Church puts upon them, but it is forbidden to go against any of the doctrines taught by the Church and contained in the deposit of faith. As proof of this statement they said that, even long after the Council of Trent, some Catholics, such as Bannes, interpreted Scripture differently from the sense of the Church and yet were never harassed, still less condemned, for so doing. Therefore, this decree is merely negative, and in no way positive.

To this argument we reply that we are free to adopt interpretations of doctrinal passages of Scripture *different from,* provided always they are *not contrary to,* the sense of the Church and the consent of the Fathers. We may go *above,* or *below,* or *beyond,* or *alongside* of, but we *must not go against,* such interpretations of the Church.

Where only one sense is possible, this distinction does not apply; but it does, or may, apply to all those passages that are capable of two or more senses, whether the senses be literal or mystical or accommodated, primary or secondary, mediate or immediate.

It will be remembered that, in certain passages of Scripture, some Catholic exegetes have admitted the existence of more than one sense, whether literal or mystical or accommodated, does not matter. According to this theory (which is neither very probable nor yet condemned) the Church may give the real and true sense of a doctrinal passage of Holy Writ. The exegete must first *positively accept* this interpretation as true; after which, *over* and *above* that sense, he may admit other senses, different from, but never contrary to, the sense defined by the Church. It is enough that those additional interpretations be not opposed either to the sense of the Church or to the consent of the Fathers or to the analogy of Catholic faith.

On its first appearance, this peculiar opinion of Jahn was promptly rejected by the great majority of Catholic writers for the following and other reasons

In perhaps all literature, whether sacred or ecclesiastical or profane, the negative form is often equivalent to a positive assertion. For instance, " Thou shalt not adore the false gods of the Gentiles," is the same as to say, " Thou shalt adore the true God of Israel." Then, too, many dogmatic definitions of councils, though negative in *form*, are clearly positive in *sense* and *substance*, and were intended to be so. Again, the Council of Trent, in the very sentence in question, makes this legislation positive, in the words: " It *belongs* to the Church to judge of the true sense and interpretation of Sacred Scripture."

Still more surprising is the fact that the very words on which Jahn bases his opinion are clearly positive in *meaning*, for the double negative, " *Nemo . . . contra*," is equivalent to the positive declaration " *Omnes . . . iuxta.*"

Again, very shortly after the Council of Trent, Pope Paul IV, in the profession of faith which public professors and many others are required to make, repeats this same regulation of Trent, but gives it in this *positive* form: "I shall interpret Sacred Scripture *according to the sense* held by the Church."[1]

Finally, to put an end to the useless discussion, the Council of the Vatican declared that "that is the true sense of Sacred Scripture which the Church has held and continues to hold." (*Constitutio Dogmatica.*)

## Seventh Proposition

*In those doctrinal passages which have received no definite interpretation from either the Church or the Fathers, the Catholic interpreter should follow the analogy, not only of Biblical, but also of Catholic faith.*

The words, "analogy of faith," are taken from St. Paul to the Romans 12. 6, where we read: κατὰ τὴν ἀναλογίαν τῆς πίστεως.

The analogy of faith may be broadly defined as the harmony or agreement existing between the truths of revealed religion. It may be of two kinds:

I. That which exists between those revealed truths which are contained in Scripture only. This is called the analogy of *Biblical* faith.

II. That which exists between *all* the truths of revealed religion, whether found in Sacred Scripture, or in *divine tradition*, or in both. This is called the analogy of *Catholic* faith.

Protestants admit only the former, which is almost identical with doctrinal Biblical parallelism.

Catholics hold both the former and the latter and

[1] "*Sacram Scripturam iuxta eum sensum quem tenuit ac tenet Sancta Mater Ecclesia interpretabor.*"

CATHOLIC PRINCIPLES 71

maintain that we must observe the analogy of the *entire* Catholic faith.

The analogy of Catholic faith consists:

1. *Formally* in the living voice and magisterium of the Church and in her daily teaching.

2. It consists *materially* and (a) *explicitly* in the authentic dogmatic decrees and symbols of faith. It consists *materially* and (b) *implicitly* in the public and universal practice of the Church.

The analogy of Catholic faith always forms a *negative,* and sometimes even a *positive,* criterion of interpretation.

1. That the analogy of Biblical faith alone is not sufficient, is clearly deduced from facts and from the principles of sound theology. Scripture is not the only channel of revelation, since it does not contain *all* the truths of revealed religion, and since many of the truths which it does contain are very obscurely expressed. Therefore, a fuller and clearer and more complete channel of revealed religion must be admitted to exist somewhere else, and this other channel of revealed truth must be the *divine tradition* of the Catholic Church.

This position is proved: (a) By *Scripture* itself, which points unmistakably to the existence of divine tradition as a concurrent channel of revelation (Rom- 16, 17; I Cor. 7, 17; II Tim. 2, 2); (b) By the unanimous consent of the *Fathers,* whom, for the sake of brevity, we need not quote. (c) By the *history* of the early Church. It is an undeniable fact that, in the beginning, Christ and his Apostles delivered *all* revealed doctrines, not in writing, but *by word of mouth, i.e.,* by oral tradition. Thus the Church was already fully equipped and organized, and was fulfilling her mission of Christianizing and civilizing the Nations for about twenty years before the first Book (Galat ? or Thess. ?) of the New Testament was written and for about sixty years before the last book of the New Testament (John's Gospel) was written.

Besides, it was never the intention of the Apostles to commit to writing all the doctrines of the Christian religion, as is manifest from the scope and character of these writings. For those writings are partial and fragmentary in character and were written for special occasions and to meet particular emergencies, with the result that there is not even one regular systematic treatise on theology in the whole of the New Testament. Neither is there anything in the occasions that produced them, nor in the writings themselves, that would indicate that any *one* of them or *all* of them together contain a complete, detailed and clear exposition of the whole religion of Christ.

2. The analogy of Catholic faith is of service both *negatively* and *positively.*

1st Rule. Every interpretation *opposed* to the analogy of Catholic faith is, by that fact alone, to be rejected as false. Thus this criterion always works negatively. A doctrine found in Sacred Scripture and a doctrine found in divine tradition both come from the same source of truth, the Holy Ghost, who cannot contradict Himself. Therefore, Sacred Scripture cannot contradict divine tradition, nor can di-

CATHOLIC PRINCIPLES 73

vine tradition contradict Sacred Scripture, nor can either of them contradict the Church.

2nd Rule. Not every interpretation that is *conformable* with the analogy of Catholic faith is therefore to be considered as the true sense of that particular passage. That is because this criterion does not always work positively. For it may very well be that an interpretation is conformable with the analogy and yet it does not give the sense of the particular passage in question, but rather the sense of some other Scriptural passage or of no scriptural passage, but the sense of some doctrine contained in divine tradition.

Still the interpreter is sometimes assisted positively in finding the true sense of Scripture by the analogy of Catholic faith. For the analogy of Catholic faith is to any passage of the Bible what the *whole* is to any of *its parts,* or what the *clear* is to the *obscure.* A part of a doctrine is naturally better understood by him who understands the entire doctrine in its various ramifications and the obscure is better seen in the light cast upon it by the clear.

This is evident also from the testimony and from the conduct of the New Testament writers. They often presuppose in their Christian reader a *previously acquired* and more complete knowlege of Christian doctrine (received from oral tradition) than they propose in their Epistles or other writings, or they refer the reader to some *subsequent oral instruction* to be given him later by the regular pastors of the Church. Of this we have many instances, among which are the following: Rom. 16, 17; II Tim. 2, 3; I Cor. 7, 17, 23;

I Cor 11, 23; I Cor. 14, 33; II Cor. 1, 18; Gala. 1, 18; Phil 4, 9, I Thess. 4, 2; II Tim 2, 2; I John 2, 12.

The following examples are too clear to need explanation:

"Stand fast and hold the traditions which you have received, whether by word of mouth or by our epistle" (II Thess 2, 14).

"Beloved, I write no new commandment to you, but an old commandment, which you had from the beginning; the old commandment is the word which you have heard" (I John 2, 7).

"I have not written to you, as if you did not know the truth, but because you know it [the truth]. . . . Let that abide in you which you heard from the beginning" (I John 2, 21, 24).

Again, "I have many things to write to you, Gaius, but I am unwilling to write them to you with pen and ink; but I hope shortly to see you and we shall speak face to face" (III John 13–14)

It is clear, then, that the New Testament writers wished what they wrote to be understood in the light of what they had taught by oral tradition or according to what they were afterwards to teach orally, or "face to face." Even today the same relationship exists between Sacred Scripture and divine tradition, or between the written and the spoken word, as existed in the days of the Apostles. Therefore, the Catholic interpreter must follow the analogy of Catholic faith.

To add greater weight to what has just been said, we quote the words of Pope Leo XIII in his Encyclical "On the Study of Sacred Scripture" Referring to the regulations of the Council of Trent regarding the interpretation of doctrinal passages of Holy Writ, he says: " By this wise decree of the Council of Trent the Church neither prevents nor restricts the pursuit of Biblical science, but protects it from error and thereby largely promotes its real progress. . . . For a wide field is still left open to the private student, in which his hermeneutical skill may display itself with signal effort and to the advantage of the Church. . . . For, on the one hand, in those passages of Scripture which have not yet received a definite interpretation, such labors, in the providence of God, may prepare the way for, and bring to maturity, the judgment of the church; on the other hand, in passages already defined, the private student may do work equally valuable, either by setting such passages more clearly before the people or by presenting them more skillfully before scholars, or by defending them more effectually from hostile attack. . . . Wherefore the first object of the Catholic commentator should be to interpret those passages which have received an authentic interpretation * * * in the same sense as the Church has explained them, and to prove by all the resources of science, that sound hermeneutical laws admit of no other interpretation than the one given by the Church. . . . In other [doctrinal] passages the analogy of [Catholic] faith should be followed and Catholic doctrine, as authoritatively proposed by the Church, should be held as the supreme law; for, seeing that the same God is the author, both of the Sacred Books and of the doctrine committed to the Church [by oral tradition], it is clearly impossible, by legitimate means, that any teachings can be extracted from the former, which can, in any way, be at variance with the latter. Hence, it follows that all interpretations are false which either make the Sacred Writers disagree with one another, or which are opposed to the doctrine of the Church . . . The Holy Fathers are of supreme authority, whenever they all interpret, in one and the same manner, any text of the Bible, as pertaining to the doctrine of faith and morals. For their unanimity clearly shows that such interpretation has come down from the Apostles as a matter of Catholic Faith. . . . The unshrinking defense of the Holy Scripture, however, does not require that we should equally uphold all the opinions which each of the Fathers or the more recent interpreters have put forth in explaining it; for it may be that, in commenting on passages where physical matters occur, they have sometimes expressed the ideas of their own times, and thus made statements which in these days have been abandoned as incorrect. Hence, in their interpretations we must carefully note what they lay down as belonging to faith or as intimately connected with faith — what they are unanimous in."

From the foregoing general principles we may deduce the following special conclusions:

1. If the Church, through the Pope or through an ecumenical council, admits a certain sense for a passage of Scripture, but does not formally or solemnly define it, the decree of Trent does not apply; for such would not be the "sense of the Church," as there understood.

2. If the Church, through the Pope or through an ecumenical council, does not formally or officially define the meaning of a text, even though there be in it question of faith and morals, but is content to quote the passage *transiently*, it is not necessary to give to such an interpretation any more weight than we would give to any similar action by the Fathers and theologians.

3. If an interpretation given to a passage of Scripture by Pope or ecumenical council refers exclusively to history, geography, geology, chronology, astronomy, or any other natural science, it does not fall within the sphere of the infallibility of the Church.

### Eighth Proposition

*An obligation in conscience rests on all, without exception, to submit to the doctrinal decisions of the Pontifical Biblical Commission, whether promulgated in the past or in the future, just as all are obliged to submit to the decrees of the Sacred Congregations, when approved by the Pope.*

This Commission was instituted October 30th, 1902, by Pope Leo XIII, for the purpose of promoting and directing Biblical studies. It is composed of several Cardinals, who alone have a deliberative voice, and of a certain number of consultors, scripturists and theologians of recognized ability in theology and Biblical science. A secretary, appointed by the Pope, takes the minutes and submits to the Holy See a report of the questions discussed and of the decisions proposed by the Commission.

The authority of these decisions was determined by Pope Pius X in a "motu proprio" which we reproduce. These decisions are neither infallible nor irreformable.

Still it is not sufficient to receive them with a mere external submission. They require the internal assent of the intellect, because they come from an accredited doctrinal authority. However, our adhesion need not be such as to exclude all possibility of error, but should be proportionate to the authority of the Commission and to the importance of the questions affected by its decisions.

Pope Pius X continues: "One is guilty of grave disobedience and of rashness if by words, whether spoken or written, one opposes these decisions, not to mention the scandal given by holding opinions contrary to those of the Holy See." [1]

From what precedes it is manifest, and from what follows below it will become still more manifest, that the Catholic Church is the only authentic and infallible interpreter of all the doctrinal parts, not only of divine tradition, but also of Sacred Scripture. This is a very fundamental and very practical exegetico-theological principle, generally called "*the Catholic principle of interpretation*" or "*the Catholic rule of faith.*" It may be thus defined:

*The Catholic Rule of Faith*

*The Catholic rule of faith is the Word of God, as*

[1] Vigouroux-Brassac, *Manuel Biblique*, T. I, *Introduction Générale*, pp. 252-253.

## CATHOLIC PRINCIPLES

*understood by the Church of God; it is the infallible Word of God, as understood by the infallible Church of God; it is the whole Word of God, both written and unwritten, both Scripture and tradition or, more fully and more accurately expressed, it is both Sacred Scripture and Divine Tradition, as interpreted by the Catholic Church.*

In this definition it is easy to see, and important to the theologian to remember, that the Catholic rule of faith contains these three elements: (1) Divine tradition; (2) Sacred Scripture, and (3) the Catholic Church.

More fully expressed it amounts to this:

1. God is the original fountainhead and *source* of all the truths of revealed religion,— of all truth.

2. Divine Tradition and Sacred Scripture are the *channel* through which the truths of revealed religion come down to us.

3. Tradition and Scripture are also called the *remote* and *passive* rule of faith.

4. The Church, which Christ has appointed to be the guardian and interpreter of Sacred Scripture and divine tradition, is called the *proximate* and *active* rule of faith.

5. The Church always interprets the doctrinal parts of Sacred Scripture in accordance with her. *divine ecclesiastical tradition.*

As we may easily suppose, this is the only rule of faith that the Catholic Church ever had or ever can have. It is an essential part of her very Constitution. It is simple, symmetrical, logical, and universal, extending to *all* times, to *all* places, to *all* persons, and to *all* the truths of revealed religion; it is universal or Catholic in every sense of the word.

# CHAPTER IV

PROTESTANT PRINCIPLES OF INTERPRETATION

## CHAPTER IV

## PROTESTANT PRINCIPLES OF INTERPRETATION

In the early ages, while many heretics abandoned, in practice, the Catholic rule of faith, still few or none of them ever formally or theoretically repudiated it or adopted another instead. To do this was left to the early reformers, who hastened to take four steps of very far reaching and disastrous consequence to themselves and to the cause of Christ:—

(1) They rejected the authority of the Catholic Church, as the only authentic interpreter of the Word

(2) They rejected divine tradition, without which the authority of Scripture can neither be established nor long maintained.

(3) They retained Scripture alone as their only rule of faith; but this is now fast slipping from their grasp.

(4) They each substituted himself, instead of the great Catholic Church, as the only proper and sufficient interpreter of Sacred Scripture

They said: " The Bible, the whole Bible, and nothing but the Bible, as interpreted by each man for and by himself, is the only rule of faith and morals "

This rule, in some form, is followed by nearly all Protestants. But as regards the special manner of applying it in interpreting Scripture, they are divided into two principal camps, and these again are divided and sub-divided into many smaller camps. The best refutation of them would be an accurate and more detailed description of them than our space can allow, showing just wherein they consist and just what they are. However, we will describe them very briefly.

1. The first Protestant rule of faith, sometimes called the pietistic rule, was generally followed by Calvinists, Anabaptists, Methodists, Wesleyans, Swedenborgians, Mennonites, Moravians, Quakers, Shakers, and by a few scattered members of other denominations, who hold that a special inspiration, or an immediate and direct revelation, or a private and personal illumination of the mind is given by the Holy Spirit to each and every Christian, teaching him what he should believe and do in all matters of faith and conduct and, especially, showing him which books are inspired and which are not inspired, and explaining to him the meaning of each and every inspired book, as far as necessary to salvation.

Their rule of faith, then, is: The Bible, and the Bible alone, as explained to each Christian by the Holy Ghost, or simply the "testimony of the Spirit." Accordingly, some who hold this rule claim to follow the guidance of the Holy Spirit, whilst retaining and *interpreting* the *Bible*. Others pretend to follow the Spirit *instead* of the Bible, which they consider *useless* and superfluous. Still others follow the Spirit in *opposition* to the Bible, which they consider *false* and misleading. On account of the many dreadful consequences to which it led, this rule has been much discredited and abandoned by the more regular Protestant denomniations.

2. *Second Protestant Principle of Interpretation*

The second Protestant rule of faith is sometimes called the rule of "private judgment" or of the "private interpretation of Scripture." It is generally followed by Episcopalians, Lutherans, Presbyterians, Congregationalists, Socinians, and, in general, by the more regular Protestant denominations. Their rule is: "The Bible, the whole Bible, and nothing but the Bible, as interpreted by *human reason.*" This, they profess, is their only rule of faith and conduct. They claim to admit nothing as a part of the Christian religion, unless they find it in the Bible; and they claim to admit everything that is found in the Bible. Both statements are false, as is easy to show.

This is sometimes called the "rational rule," because they claim that reason is the only means or instrument that we have to interpret Sacred Scripture. However, they who follow this rule are divided into two general classes, and these are again divided and sub-divided into many minor classes:

(a) Some of them say that "*individual* human reason" alone is a sufficient interpreter of Scripture. They maintain that the sense of Scripture is so plain, so clear, so obvious, so transparent, that any man, no matter how ignorant he may be, is able to understand Scripture properly. Thus, then, "The Bible, and the Bible alone, as understood by anybody, even by the most ignorant member of the human race, is the true rule of faith and conduct."

(b) Others hold that individual human reason alone is not sufficient, but that "*collective* human reason" is the only proper interpreter of Scripture. They maintain that the sense of Scripture is not so plain, not so clear, not so obvious, not so transparent, that the unaided reasoning powers of the ignorant man are sufficient to enable him, ever and always, to discover the true sense of Scripture; but that, on the contrary, the sense of Scripture is often so very obscure that, in order to discover it with certainty, he needs the assistance of human reason *in general,* the reason of the *many,* the reason of *mankind* at large, that is, *collective* human reason.

But here these are again sub-divided into two groups: (1) Some hold that the assistance to be given to individual reason should be *literary, scientific* and *Biblical;* (2) Others maintain that it should be *ecclesiastical* and *religious.* In other words:

1) The former hold that the reasoning faculties of the individual, in order to understand Scripture properly, should be trained, educated, instructed, enlightened, and supplied with some knowledge of higher criticism, hermeneutics, archæology, Biblical exegesis, Biblical philosophy, general literature and ancient languages, and perhaps a very general knowledge of chemistry, physics, mechanics, mathematics, geology and astronomy, all of which are sometimes referred to in Scripture.

So their rule of faith is: " The Bible, and the Bible

alone, as interpreted by educated, enlightened, collective human reason." As is evident, this rule is not made for the many, but for the select *few;* not for the multitude, but only for the *learned,* the *scholarly,* and the *wealthy.* For how can the poor man ever get the time and the money and the leisure to learn all those sciences or any one of them?

2) Those of the second group contend that a knowledge of these and other natural sciences, while all very good in a way, is neither necessary nor sufficient. For these and other such sciences, after all, are only *natural,* and cannot explain the sense of Sacred Scripture, which is something *divine,* something full of mysteries, full of the "deep things of God," and that, therefore, it lies beyond the reach of unaided natural reason.

So they require that individual human reason, while searching for the sense of the Scripture, should be assisted and directed by the *Church;* not perhaps by their own little Church, but by the Catholic Church; not by the great Catholic Church of to-day, but by the Catholic Church of the early ages, some of whose interpretations of Scripture may be found in the decrees of the first five or six general councils and in the writings of the early Fathers.

But, since they have no authentic or infallible interpretation of the decrees of those early councils, nor of the writings of those primitive Fathers, they who follow this rule are compelled to interpret those writings as best they can. But, as is evident, this is only another instance of private judgment in religious matters; only, in this particular case, the private judgment is exercised, not on Sacred Scripture, but on the Divine Tradition of the Church; and this is the same old error under a new form.

They say they appeal to the Church of the early ages to explain the Divine Tradition of the Church. Useless appeal; for that Church is dead and gone and can entertain no appeal. But, so far as the early Church still continues to exist and so far as it still survives, it survives in the Catholic Church of to-day and is identical with her in all her teachings.

This last method of applying the rule of private judgment is much followed in the Episcopal or Anglican Church, often called the Church of England, and especially in that branch of it which is called the High Church. This is the nearest approach, in appearance, to the Catholic rule of faith and interpretation.

Once we have a clear concept of the intrinsic nature of the various Protestant methods of interpreting Scripture, it becomes *a priori* manifest that not one of them can be the authentic and infallible interpreter of Scripture The same conclusion follows, still more clearly, *a posteriori,* or from their results, which have produced endless confusion and discord among Protestants themselves.

We may be sure that it was not by any of these Protestant methods of interpretation, nor by any special or profound study of the Scriptures that the " Reformation " was first established or continued to exist.

Rather, it was in consequence of the ignorance and

indifference of the people, the politics of princes and potentates, and the avarice of the nobility, who saw in it an opportunity to enrich themselves by the plunder of Church property.

We may go a step farther and affirm that there is no evidence to prove that anyone, whether Protestant or non-Protestant, ever formed his religious creed out of the Bible and by the exclusive use of the rule of private judgment or private interpretation. On the contrary, the truth is that, from their early childhood, Protestants are taught the use of creeds and catechisms; they are carefully tutored in the doctrines of their respective denominations, long before they have ever read the Bible; they are guided by their parents and teachers; they are influenced by the opinions and example of those among whom they live and with whom they are in daily contact; and thus they are led to believe that they have learned from the Bible what they really have learned from their surroundings and from what they have breathed in from the atmosphere in which they are immersed. Thus, often, they are Protestants long before they have read the Bible, and even before they have learned or know how to read at all. Some particular texts of Scripture are strongly impressed upon their minds and other texts, of an apparently different meaning, are kept out of their sight or are glossed over; and, above all, it is steadily and persistently inculcated on their minds that their religion is built exclusively on Scripture and that they are Bible Christians. Hence, when they read the Bible, they really imagine that they find in its pages what they have been taught to believe was there. For instance, the Anglicans see in Scripture that Baptism is necessary to infants, while the Baptists read there that Baptism is useless and even harmful to their salvation. (Milner, *End of Religious Controversy,* VIIIth Letter.)

All this is very inconsistent and even self-contradictory. For, among those who profess to get their religion out of the Bible alone, there ought to be no articles of faith, no symbols, no catechisms, no sermons and no other sources of religious instruction than the Bible and the Bible only, or, if there are to be such things, they ought to be formulated and taught by the Catholic Church.

Luther maintained, in theory, the rule, not of collective but of individual private judgment in the interpretation of Scripture; but in practice he was often compelled to abandon it. His own disciples followed the very rule which he himself had so loudly proclaimed as the true rule, proved, from the clearest texts of Scripture, that, in many things, Luther himself was in error, and that the Reformation needed reforming.

He had let down the bars and was powerless to prevent his disciples from following out his own rule to its logical conclusion. They preached against him and against one another with the utmost virulence, while one and all professed to ground their doctrine and conduct on the Bible and the Bible only, and boasted that they interpreted it in accordance with the fundamental rule of private judgment, which Luther himself had taught them to follow.

## PROTESTANT PRINCIPLES

In their own interest, the civil rulers and the leaders of the Reformation began to hold synods and assemblies, consistories and convocations; they published creeds and symbols, catechisms and professions of faith, and adopted other more drastic methods, the purpose of which was to obtain and maintain at least an external uniformity of belief among the members of each denomination or within the limits of each kingdom or state. But it was like the unity of a tenement house.

In fact, the most enlightened Protestants find themselves in an awkward dilemma and are obliged to say and to unsay many things to the amusement of some and the pity of others They cannot abandon the rule of the Bible alone, as explained by each one for himself, without proclaiming to the world their guilt in refusing to hear the true Church; and they cannot adhere to the rule of the Bible alone, without opening the flood-gates of impiety and infidelity and endless discord upon their own denomination. (Milner, *End of Religious Controversy*, VIIIth Letter.)

The leaders of the movement had placed the cause, and then attempted to prevent its unavoidable effects, by obliging ministers, professors, and even the people to take an oath not to follow the rule (the Bible), but, instead, to follow the creeds and the professions of faith which had been drawn up and adopted by fallible men like themselves. The leaders imposed fines and imprisonment, and endeavored to force an external compliance by means of the rack, the ax, and the fagot In consequence, an intense reign of terror prevailed in most Protestant countries.

To give, in theory and with one hand, the right of private interpretation to every man, and then, in practice and with the other hand to take it away again, was so manifestly contradictory and outrageous that new sects without number swarmed everywhere and faith in Christianity was badly shaken.

Lest all this be misunderstood, we take the precaution to say that creeds and catechisms and councils and consistories are perfectly in line with the Catholic rule of faith, because, decades before the New Testament was written, Christ our Lord had appointed His Church to preach His gospel to all nations, and had left her free to choose her own methods of doing her own work, according to the circumstances of times, places and persons, and has blessed her with success in the doing.

# CHAPTER V

# RATIONALISTIC PRINCIPLES OF INTERPRETATION

# CHAPTER V

# RATIONALISTIC PRINCIPLES OF INTERPRETATION

1. *Socinianism*

Out of all the confusion caused by the adoption of the Protestant rule of faith, there arose another phase of religious liberty called Socinianism. *Laelius Socinus* (b.1525–d. 1562) and *Faustus Socinus* (b. 1534–d. 1604), uncle and nephew, were expelled from Switzerland because of their "advanced" views, especially on the Holy Trinity. They taught that the mysteries and miracles related in Scripture may be admitted, but only so far as they are shown to agree with philosophical principles or scientific conclusions. They denied emphatically the Trinity of Persons in God and, for this reason, were often called Unitarians. They retained the traditional theological terminology, that is, the ecclesiastical use of words, if only *pro forma*, but perverted their meaning Thus they admitted a Trinity in God of Father, Son, and Holy Ghost,— not, however, as distinct persons, but only as divine impersonal attributes The Father is Power, the Son is Wisdom, the Holy Ghost is simply Goodness. They also admit that the Word of God, or Logos, became incarnate in man, not by a personal, substantial or hypostatic union, but only by a moral or accidental union of God with man. God, they say, is thus incarnate, not merely in an individual man, in Christ our Lord, but in collective humanity, in all good men, by a mere moral union of grace. It is most evident that Socinianism was mere Naturalism awkwardly concealed behind or under a Christian mask.

These ideas made their way to England, and, about 1660, Hume, Hobbes, and Bolingbroke openly denied mysteries, revelations, miracles, prophesies, inspiration, and even the human authority of Scripture.

From England the virus crossed the Channel into France and produced Diderot, Rousseau, Voltaire, the Encyclopedists, and, finally, the French Revolution.

From France it crossed the Rhine into Germany, where it took up its permanent abode, developed gigantic proportions, assumed for the first time a systematic form and a scientific shape, was cultivated seriously like any other science, and soon received the name of Rationalism,— Biblical Rationalism.

The English Deists and French infidels were extreme, irreverent, rabid; they denied everything, they ridiculed everything. But the German Rationalists were, and still are, outwardly moderate, more self-restrained, more serious, more insinuating, more reverential and more dangerous. They admit Scripture; they speak of it with respect; they praise it above all other books; but, at the same time, they explain it in such a way as to rob it of its inspired, supernatural character and place it on a level with all other merely human literary productions.

## 2. *Rationalism*

It is necessary to note the very broad distinction between Protestant and Rationalistic principles of Biblical hermeneutics.

(1) The two agree in this, that both reject the Catholic Church as the authentic interpreter of Scripture, and make reason the only sufficient guide, not only in the interpretation of Scripture, but also in all other things pertaining to religion.

(2) But they differ in this, that Protestants, at least so-called orthodox Protestants, make reason the sole judge, but only in a hermeneutical sense, that is to say, they hold that reason alone should be left to discover which is the real sense intended by the sacred writer; but, this sense once discovered, they maintain that reason is no longer free to reject it, but must accept it on the authority of God who reveals it,— must accept it, even though it should contain revelations of mysteries, or accounts of miracles and prophecies, and what-not supernatural. All this, because orthodox Protestants are supposed to admit the inspiration and the consequent credibility of Scripture.

On the other hand, the Rationalists go so far as to make individual reason the only supreme judge of truth in *all* things. Reason alone must decide, not only which is the real sense of Scripture,— that is, which is the sense intended by the inspired writer,— but also whether that sense, intended by the sacred writer, is true in itself, is objectively true and conformable with the facts or the theories in the case. In other words, reason must decide whether that sense should be accepted as true or rejected as false. Briefly, Rationalists deny the inspiration and the infallibility of Scripture. Much more, they deny everything supernatural, whether in Scripture or out of Scripture. Let us explain this more in detail.

Rationalism may be defined, in general, as the system or theory which assigns *undue importance* to *reason* in human affairs, or puts *excessive reliance* on *human reason* alone in matters of opinion and practice, independently of authority.

Thus, Rationalism makes reason the only guide to truth and the only *source* in which a knowledge of truth originates and from which it emanates. Rationalism makes reason the court of final appeal in *all* things.

Rationalism is of many kinds, but chiefly (1) Philosophical, (2) Theological, (3) Biblical.

1. *Philosophical* Rationalism is the system which makes reason the only norm or criterion of truth, the only guide to truth, the only source of truth in general, and the supreme arbiter and judge of all truth of all kinds, *as distinct from both Sensism and Experimentalism*. It is the theory of *a priori* ideas and principles.

2. *Theological* Rationalism is the system or theory of those who deduce all their religious opinions ultimately and exclusively from reason, *as distinct from supernatural revelation*. It is the doctrine of those who reject the entire supernatural order and rely exclusively on human reason as the only criterion and

RATIONALISTIC PRINCIPLES 99

the only source of all our knowledge of *morals and religion.*

3. *Biblical* Rationalism, also called Historico-Critico-Exegetical Rationalism, regards the exegesis of Scripture and is, as the name implies, the theory of those who maintain that *the Bible is in no true sense the Word of God,* that it contains no divine supernatural revelation, especially of mysteries, and that, consequently, it is to be interpreted like any other mere human book, or like any other mere profane literary production, that is, in accordance with the principles of rational hermeneutics. All this in general.

Biblical Rationalism may be briefly summarized under the following three heads: (1) Deistic, (2) Theistic, (3) Semi-Christian.

1. The *Deistic* form of Rationalism denies the existence of mysteries and, consequently, the possibility of the revelation of mysteries. It denies also the existence of miracles and prophecies, which are the ordinary criteria of supernatural revelation. It denies all else supernatural.

2. The *Theistic* form of Rationalism admits the *possibility* and even the *existence* of a supernatural revelation and that such revelation is to be found in Scripture. But, at the same time, it holds that the truths thus supernaturally revealed are truths which reason not only can understand, can comprehend, and can even prove to be true, after they have once been revealed, but which reason could have discovered, if left to itself, or if it took the time and trouble necessary to discover them. Reason could, and eventually would,

have discovered them in the long run, though slowly and with difficulty. With revelation, these things are discovered more easily and quickly. A traveler can go across the country from station to station on foot; he can go much faster and more comfortably in a parlor car or on an express train.

Such revelation, considered actively in its cause and in its manner, is supernatural; considered passively, for the truths revealed, it is natural.

3. The *Semi-Christian* form of Rationalism teaches that many truths revealed in Scripture cannot be discovered by reason alone without supernatural revelation; but that, after they have been revealed, reason can understand and explain them according to the well-established principles of philosophy and can positively establish their conformity with reason. In this case, such truths are raised from the sphere of faith or belief to the sphere of science or knowledge. Yet, until their conformity with reason has been established, they are to be received on authority; but if, on examination, such teachings are found to be non-conformable with reason, they are to be rejected as false; for reason is the only norm and source of truth, the supreme arbiter of truth.

The many extravagant vagaries of Biblical Rationalism will be better understood, if we can, in some way, classify them and summarize them, much as follows:

There is in Scripture a threefold supernatural element or content, (1) a dogmatic, (2) a moral, and (3) a historical

1) The supernatural *dogmatic* element in Scripture

consists of abstract, speculative truths called *mysteries*, which surpass the capacity of the human intellect either to discover them or to comprehend them, even after they have been revealed, *e.g.*, the holy Trinity.

2) The supernatural *moral* element in Scripture consists of *laws, precepts,* and *counsels* which belong to the supernatural order of redemption and require supernatural grace to perform them, *e g ,* love for one's enemies.

3) The supernatural *historical* element consists of certain facts which surpass the power and the order of all created nature to produce them.

(a) Those facts which surpass the power and the order of all *physical* nature are called *miracles, e g.,* to raise the dead.

(b) Those facts which surpass the power and the order of the human *intellect* and which regard the occurrence of free, future, contingent events are miracles of the moral order and are called *prophecies*

Therefore, there are, in general, only three systems of Rationalistic hermeneutics, with their various divisions and sub-divisions, one for each kind of supernatural element or content in the Bible, as just described. They are:

1) Semler's system of *practical dogmatic* accommodation, which was intended to eliminate from Scripture the supernatural dogmatic element.

2) Kant's system of *moral* interpretation, which was intended to eliminate from Scripture the supernatural moral element.

3) (a) The system of *psychological* interpretation

invented by Paulus; and (b) the system of *mythical* interpretation invented by Strauss; and (c) the system of *legendary* interpretation urged by Renan, were all intended to eliminate from Scripture the supernatural historical element, that is to say, miracles and prophesies. We shall discuss them in order, and as briefly as consistent with clearness.[1]

A) *The System of Positive Dogmatic Accommodation* was developed by J. S. Semler of Halle. According to Semler (b. 1721–d. 1791) nothing can be admitted as true, if it pretends to exceed the limits of pure reason. Thus, mysteries, miracles, prophecies, revelations, inspiration, the holy Trinity, the divinity of Christ, the resurrection from the dead, grace, etc., in fact, the entire super-natural order should be rejected as false.

Many of the doctrines just mentioned were prevalent in Palestine at the time of Christ and His Apostles. Accordingly, Semler maintained that, in order to gain the good will of the Jews and ultimately to induce them to accept His claims to Messiahship, Christ, by what is called *positive dogmatic accommodation,* outwardly approved those doctrines and adopted them as His own, though He knew well that they were false.

To avoid equivocation in this matter we shall define what is meant, in general, by accommodation and shall explain the difference between its various kinds. There are, in general, two kinds of accommodation, 1) the esthetical and 2) the practical.

[1] For a more ample discussion of this topic the student may consult the General Introductions of Chauvin, pp. 605–625, Gigot, pp. 458–464; Dixon, pp. 222 ff.; Ubaldi, and others.

## RATIONALISTIC PRINCIPLES

1. The *Esthetical* accommodated sense we have already explained. It is not the sense of Sacred Scripture; it is the sense of the interpreter of Scripture It is, however, of such a sort that, on account of some analogy, it can be fittingly adapted to Sacred Scripture. In esthetical accommodation there is question of borrowing the *words* of another in which to clothe one's own ideas; but the ideas of the writer, whose words are quoted, are not borrowed, are not appropriated.

2. *Practical* accommodation, which is the only one under consideration here, and in which the *thoughts* of another are borrowed, is a way of acting or speaking in which a person does something or omits something in order to conform or adapt himself to others.

There are principally three kinds of practical accommodation, 1) the *moral*, 2) the *pedagogical*, 3) the *dogmatic*. The difference between them depends on the character or the nature of the action done or omitted.

1) The practical *moral* accommodation is one by which a person performs an action that is not commanded, or omits an action that is not forbidden, in order to adapt himself to the *weak conscience* of others or to avoid scandal. St. Paul, for instance, would not eat meat offered to idols, if it gave scandal to the weaker brethren. (Acts 6, 3; 21, 20–26; I Corinthians 8, 9 to 13).

2) Practical *pedagogical* accommodation is that by which a teacher adapts himself and his methods of teaching to the *mental calibre,* or intellectual capacity, or grade of instruction of his hearers in all that re-

gards the choice or selection of topics, the order and arrangement of materials and the method of exposition.

Every good teacher constantly accommodates himself pedagogically. That is why higher mathematics and transcendental philosophy are not taught to children in the elementary schools, but are reserved for other times and places and persons. (Matthew 13, 10; John 16, 12–14; Hebrews 5, 11–14).

3) Practical *dogmatical* accommodation is that by which a person accommodates his *teachings* to the infirmity of others. It is of two kinds: a) negative and b) positive.

a) *Negative* dogmatic accommodation is that by which a teacher, for motives of prudence, *permits* some imperfect, or even false notions, to remain in the minds of his pupils and *abstains* from immediately eradicating them, but at the same time, says nothing that could be considered as an approval of them.

b) *Positive* dogmatic accommodation is that by which a person not only tolerates, not only permits, but also praises, confirms, approves and outwardly adopts as his own the errors and prejudices of others, though he himself internally does not believe in them. It is, of course, understood that the teacher does *not really*, but *only apparently*, adopt such errors as his own. If he really believed in the doctrines, it would be a case of *false belief*, but not a case of *accommodation*.

Now, not only esthetical, but also practical accommodation of the three kinds already mentioned (*i.e.*, moral, pedagogical and negative dogmatic) are all

## RATIONALISTIC PRINCIPLES

lawful in their proper time and place and when practiced with due precaution. They were all used even by our Lord himself and by His Apostles.

Yet this admission does not help Semler and his school, because they defend *positive* dogmatic accommodation, which, we contend, is ever and always forbidden. We deny that Christ or His Apostles ever encouraged it, or in any way sanctioned it either by their words or by their example. And no one has yet proved the contrary.

Since Semler's whole system of accommodation is based upon the gratuitous supposition that Christ *did* accommodate, as he says, and since it is absolutely certain that Christ *did not* thus accommodate, the system, having no foundation in fact to rest upon, falls to the ground of its own weight.

B) *The system of moral interpretation* was introduced by Emmanuel Kant (b. 1724–d. 1804). Kant holds (a) that all religion consists exclusively of the ethical law, of the moral law of nature, as known to pure reason, to unaided human reason; (b) that there is and there can be only one true religion, the religion of nature; for nature and the ethical law of nature are universal and the same for all men; (c) that all so-called revealed religions are good, but only so far as they reproduce some precepts of the one religion of nature, of the moral law. Therefore, everything supernatural, whether dogmatic, moral or historical, found in the so-called revealed religions of the world, should be rejected either as positively false or, at least, as useless. Thus religion, the religion of pure reason, the only religion that Kant admits, is based on morality alone,— not on supernatural, but on natural morality, upon natural ethics.

Therefore, no matter what violence is done to the text, no matter how repugnant it may be to the context, or to the scope of the writer, or to the subject matter of the book, the natural moral sense, as known to pure reason, is ever and always to be sought.

Kant's system of interpretation rests on the hypothesis that religion consists solely of moral principles. But this hypothesis is not only gratuitous, for he makes no attempt to prove it, but it is also positively false. Kant mistakes a part for the whole. As Kant makes *no attempt* to prove his absurd and gratuitous assertions, we can well afford to deny them just as gratuitously.

C) *The system of psychological or naturalistic interpretation* advocated by Paulus (b. 1761–d. 1851) is the most arbitrary and the most violent that can well be imagined. His idea is that, in the accounts of the gospel miracles, we should carefully distinguish two very different elements: (a) the objective element and (b) the subjective element. The *objective* element is the *fact* in the case; it is what took place; it is what occurred. For, surely, he says something happened, whatever it was. Opinions may vary about its origin, cause, nature or purpose. But, whatever it was, something happened. The *subjective* element is the *opinion* entertained about that fact; it is the judgment formed about that event, either by the original witnesses, or by the narrator of the event, or by subsequent readers of the narrative. Some of these misunderstood either the cause, or the purpose, or the nature of the event and exaggerated it into the miraculous.

In theory and after a fashion, Paulus admits the *historical truthfulness* of the gospel narrative, but interprets it in such a way as to exclude from it everything supernatural, whether doctrinal, moral or historical.

For instance, Paulus says: Lazarus did not die, but had only swooned. Christ happened to come to the sepulchre just at the opportune moment, found his friend already revived or reviving, and called him forth from the tomb. Paulus wants to convey the impression that the whole incident was staged for effect, and that it was a collusion between Christ and Lazarus for the purpose of enhancing the authority of the Messiah.

Another instance: the man born blind was cured. That is a *fact* certified to by competent witnesses, and there is no reason to doubt it. But, as to the cause of the cure, the witnesses really knew nothing about that; however, it is a mistake to suppose that it was produced by a miracle. The cure must have been brought about by some natural cause, by some medicine known to Oriental oculists and to Christ who was a great physician.

Strange that this marvellous medicine, a medicine capable of giving sight to an adult who had been blind all his life, in fact to a man who had been born blind, should be so thoroughly lost as to be unknown to modern medical science.

The psychological system of Paulus is manifestly arbitrary, false and absurd and does violence to the most obvious meaning of Scripture and to the most fundamental principles of hermeneutics. If such a method may be applied to the gospels, there is no reason why it should not be applied to any or all of the historical writings of ancient and modern times.

The whole system rests on the gratuitous assumption that the supernatural is impossible. When challenged to prove some of his absurd hypotheses, Paulus pretended to be surprised that he should be expected to prove anything or to do more than assert his impressions. Was not his bare word sufficient to upset the faith of the Christian world? Strauss, a former pupil of Paulus, dealt the death blow to this whole theory.

D) *The system of mythical interpretation* was introduced by Eichhorn, and developed by Baur and Strauss. J. G. Eichhorn (b. 1752–d. 1827), professor at Göttingen, admitted myths in the early chapters of *Genesis,* but further he refused to go. Others extended the theory to all the books of the *Old Testament.* F. C. Baur (b. 1792–d. 1860), professor at Tübingen, was the first to apply this theory to the *New Testament.* D. F. Strauss (b. 1808–d. 1874) carried it to the greatest extremes and boldly applied it to the *principal events in the life of our Lord* in the gospels. Strauss teaches that the life of Christ, as related in the gospels, is not historical, but that His marvellous birth, infancy, miracles, prophecies, resurrection from the dead and ascension into Heaven are all fictions, are all so many myths. He admits that contemporary writers never write myths and that, if the gospels were written by writers contemporary with the events related in them, their contents would be, not mythical, but historical. He says that myths take time, a long time, to grow and that a certain remoteness in time is necessary to their formation and gradual development

Accordingly, Strauss maintained that the gospels were written between A. D. 150 and 175. In that interval of 120 or 140 years, between the death of Christ and the composition of the gospels, these myths, which were suggested by the Messianic prophecies of the Old Testament, were gradually developed and innocently incorporated into the gospels.

Thus, while denying the supernatural element in the gospels, Strauss *never would accuse* the *evangelists*, whoever they were, of *intentional fabrication* or of subjective conscious falsehood. They were *deceived*, he said; they wrote so long after the occurrence of the events related that they were not conscious of the mythical character of what they wrote. They had inherited it from the distant past and believed that it was all right.

Strauss gratuitously took it for granted that the gospels contained myths, so as to have an opportunity for bringing the date of their composition down to A D. 150 or 175, and to destroy or very much diminish their authority. He also gratuitously took it for granted that the gospels were not written before A. D. 150 or

175, so as to have an excuse for maintaining that they contained myths and so as to destroy or seriously diminish their authority.

Strauss never made any serious attempt to prove either hypothesis.

No very satisfactory definition of the word myth has yet been formed. Still, the word may be defined, with sufficient accuracy for practical purposes, as the *narrative* of some *supposedly historical event,* or as the *expression* of some *philosophical or religious idea* under a form absolutely historical, though absolutely false. In the fable and parable, the form of narrative is not absolutely historical, and the reader can always discover, and is supposed to discover, that the narrative is fictitious and that the writer never intended that it should be understood literally, but only as a sign or figure of something else. But in the myth, the form of the narrative is so *absolutely historical* that the reader never would discover the difference and would naturally continue to interpret the narrative as real history, unless philosophical considerations intervened to withhold him from so doing,— which is not always the case.

Then, according to Strauss and his school, it took philosophical considerations from 2000 to 3000 years to discover that certain narratives in the Bible are mythical, though, down to his day, all generations of Bible readers took them for historical.

Perhaps the following definition of the myth may help to make the idea still clearer to the reader. " The myth is a fictitious and conjectural narrative presented as historical, but without any basis in fact. It is the *creation of a fact out of an idea.* The legend is the discovery of an idea in a fact. The myth is purely the work of imagination; the legend has some basis in fact." (*New Standard Dictionary;* see Trench, *Parables,* Chap. II, for the difference between myth, legend, parable and fable.)

"The myth simply invents, imagines, creates its facts. In the myth, the ideal and the real are identified, the subjective and the objective are inseparably blended." The conclusion is, no matter how innocently intended by the myth-maker, the result for us is practically the same, the myth in itself is a falsehood.

Myths are found, as Strauss himself acknowledges, only in an *unhistorical* age and at a time when the people forming them are in their infancy as a nation.

But, in the time of Christ, the Jews had already passed out of their infantile stage perhaps thousands of years before.

Also, to any reasonable man, it must appear absolutely fatal to the theory of Strauss to know that the time of Christ was the most historical age of all antiquity. For Christ wrought His wonderful works, and His Apostles and their immediate disciples wrote them down in the most enlightened period of Greek and Roman history, *i.e.,* in the age of the great historians, Livy, Tacitus, Suetonius, and Josephus Flavius, in the age when Greek and Roman civilization, literature, art, and general culture had reached their highest stage of development; after which they began to decline.

But we need not enter here upon a refutation of this absurd system, partly because Strauss never made any serious attempt to prove his arbitrary assumptions, and partly because those assumptions have been positively and directly refuted by men of most scholarly attainments. For, since the time of Strauss, even more than ever before, it has been proved in the most scientific and critical fashion, and even by men of very "advanced" views, that the gospels are the genuine works of the Apostles and of their disciples and were written about the middle of the first century of the Christian era. All this means that they were published to the world too soon for the occurrence of the events related in them to contain any trace of such myths, as Strauss gratuitously asserts. St. John, in extreme old age, wrote his gospel, later than the others, but he was an eye-witness of the facts which he relates. Therefore, this system, like those that preceded it, resting on no foundation in fact, falls to the ground of its own weight. There are but few who follow it at the present time.

E) *The system of legendary interpretation* was offered by E. Renan (b. 1823–d 1892) as a substitute for Strauss' mythical theory.

The difference between the myth and the legend, as we have already seen, is that the myth is "pure and absolute imagination without any basis in fact," whereas "the legend is a narrative based on tradition with some, though slight, intermixture of fact."

Renan's manner of discussing some of the most serious topics of religion is so flippant and whimsical as to lead many of his readers to suspect that he had no convictions on such matters. His popularity is chiefly the result of superficial learning combined with frequent and varied blasphemies expressed in the most captivating style.

If the reader will examine them carefully, he will observe that most of these rationalistic theories mutually exclude and destroy one another.

1. Strauss, one of his pupils, thoroughly refutes the psychological theory of Paulus and covers it with ridicule.

2. Baur, one of his pupils, proves conclusively that the mythological theory of Strauss is manifestly opposed to the facts in the case and is altogether absurd.

3. Renan, assisted by many others, proved that the " tendency theory " of Baur has no foundation in fact to rest upon and many of Baur's own school have been forced by the more conservative Christian scholarship of Europe to abandon his theory as false and gratuitous.

4. Renan, on the contrary, held the legendary theory, substituting the legend for the myth, the less objectionable for the more objectionable, so as not to offend his more orthodox French and English readers. His method of interpretation is lawless, flighty, capricious and whimsical in the extreme. It was based on gratuitous assumptions, and was floated for awhile by his charming style of language, but is not worthy of any serious attempt at refutation.

# CHAPTER VI

## DIVINE TRADITION AN ESSENTIAL PART OF THE CATHOLIC PRINCIPLE OF HERMENEUTICS

## CHAPTER VI

## DIVINE TRADITION AN ESSENTIAL PART OF THE CATHOLIC PRINCIPLE OF HERMENEUTICS

Divine ecclesiastical tradition is of prime importance in Catholic theology. It is the only adequate means of proving either the inspiration or the canonicity of the Sacred Books. It is also an essential element both in the Catholic rule of faith and in the Catholic principle of interpretation (which we are now discussing): for, without it, we cannot know for certain the meaning of the doctrinal contents of the inspired books. It is usually discussed in fundamental dogmatic theology. But as some of our readers may not yet have seen it there, and others of them may never see it either there or elsewhere, we consider it our duty both to the student and to the general reader to discuss it here as fully as space will allow.

### Definition

The word *tradition* has a great variety of meanings, and is often used loosely and without the necessary qualifying adjectives to make its meaning, in a given case, clear and precise.

Still, there is this advantage in it that all its various meanings are only so many divisions or subdivisions of the one general sense, and this general sense is clearly and invariably based on the root or etymology of the word. For the sake of those readers who have not studied theology, let us explain the meaning of the word somewhat in detail.

The word tradition (*paradosis*) is composed of two Latin words, "*tra*," short for "*trans*," which means *over, across, down, along;* and "*do*," *give* or *convey*, — and means transmission or handing along or handing down from one to another. This general meaning underlies its use in all cases.

Still, some traditions are not easily classified because they overlap and blend into one. Some, also, do not concern us here, yet we mention them just to round out and to complete the meaning of the word.

### Division

The following are some of the principal divisions of tradition, along with the *basis* or *ground* of each distinction:

Traditions are,

1. In character, (a) profane or (b) theological;
2. In substance, (a) material or (b) immaterial;
3. In form, (a) written or (b) oral;
4. In voice, (a) active or (b) passive,
5. In extent, (a) broad or (b) narrow;
6. In origin, (a) human or (b) ecclesiastical or (c) Apostolic or (d) divine.

We shall explain them briefly in order, but are concerned, chiefly, with the last member of each pair.

In *character*, traditions are either, (a) profane or (b) theological. The difference is obvious.

1. In speaking of *profane* or worldly matters, the word tradition is very variously used. For instance: in *legal* documents the word tradition often denotes the formal act of transferring property from one person to another; also the title-deeds by which the transfer is made. In many other circumstances, civil, military, academic, etc., the word tradition often means either the formal delivery of the symbols of office, or the conferring of privileges or titles of nobility by letters patent, the conferring of various honors by decorations or of academic degrees by diplomas, or of ordination by the "*traditio instrumentorum.*" Also in the *fine arts* generally (painting, sculpture, the drama), in universities and professional schools (as of law, medicine, and theology) and in similar institutions, the word tradition is often and properly used to express the accumulated knowledge, wisdom, taste, skill, experience, customs and ways and means and methods of doing things, handed down through successive generations of artists, authors, actors, teachers, officials, magistrates. Law courts and medical associations, in fact, every profession has its traditions, and many great institutions are governed almost entirely by their traditions. Daniel Webster writes: " Tradition . . . hands down the practical arts with more precision and fidelity than can be transmitted by books." (*Private*

*Correspondence,* Vol. II, p. 408.) In what follows we are chiefly concerned with *theological tradition.*

2) The *object* handed down to us by tradition may be either: (a) a material, concrete thing, such as a book, a diploma, a Bible, a piece of real estate; or (b) an immaterial, abstract object, such as ideas, opinions, truths, things of the mind, which may be considered either collectively or individually and one by one. In what follows we are concerned chiefly with the *immaterial* or abstract objects of tradition.

3) As regards their *form* or the *manner* and *means* of conveying them, theological traditions may be transmitted either, (a) in writing, or (b) by word of mouth. The difference is evident. In what follows we are concerned chiefly, though not exclusively, with *oral* tradition.

4) In *voice,* oral tradition (considered as just described) may be either (a) active and subjective, or (b) passive and objective.

(a) Taken in its *active* sense, tradition is the *act* of transmitting from one person to another. It is the *process* of communicating ideas, thoughts, knowledge, opinions, customs, doctrines, truths from generation to generation by word of mouth only, or by example.

(b) Taken in its *passive* sense, tradition is the *result* of the act just described; it is the *effect* of that cause; it is the *thing* which has been handed down from one to another. More precisely, it is the collection of the truths of faith and morals, originally taught by Christ to and through His Apostles, and then handed along

CATHOLIC DOCTRINE OF TRADITION 121

down through the ages, by word of mouth or by example. It may be found also in the works of the Church Fathers and in the decrees of popes and councils In what follows we are concerned with tradition chiefly, though not exclusively, in its *passive* sense.

5) In extent passive tradition may be taken in either of two senses: (a) broad, or (b) narrow.

(a) Taken in its *broadest* sense, passive tradition includes *all* the truths of revealed religion, whether transmitted in *writing*, as in the Sacred Books, or handed down by *word of mouth*, or by example, as in Oral Tradition

Here it is very important to remember that even Sacred Scripture is a part of divine tradition, when taken in this broad sense of the word; for, as is manifest on reflection, even Scripture itself, like so many other things, has been floated down to us from the days of the Apostles on this great, broad stream of oral tradition, and could not have reached us by any other means.

(b) Taken in its *narrow* sense, divine tradition includes, not Sacred Scripture, but *only those truths* of revealed religion which were originally taught by Christ and His Apostles, and which have been safely handed down to us orally, through successive generations of the legitimate pastors of the Church, under the guidance of the Holy Ghost. In this sense, tradition may have been subsequently committed to writing in the works of the Fathers, and in the decrees of Popes and councils, though not in Sacred Scripture. In what follows we are concerned with tradition chiefly in this narrow sense, that is, as distinct from Sacred Scripture.

It is necessary to have a clear idea of what is meant by, especially, the divine tradition on which the Church depends as the source of all her doctrines of faith and morals. The topic is very important and complicated, yet we hope to make it clear by explaining positively what each kind of tradition is and also by explaining negatively what it is not. Each variety of tradition should be carefully distinguished by its appropriate epithet or adjective.

6) As to their *origin* or *source,* there are principally four kinds of tradition: (1) human, (2) ecclesiastical, (3) Apostolic, (4) divine. Let us see positively what they are, as follows:

1. Some traditions are called *human,* because they originated with men and have, at most, merely human authority. They are sometimes popular stories, beliefs, usages, customs, myths, fables, legends, narratives or accounts of things apparently historical in character, and sometimes originating no one knows when, where, how or why, and all transmitted by word of mouth by the people. At the same time, there are many human traditions clearly traceable to their real origin and forming *perfectly reliable* sources of historical information.

2. Some traditions are called *ecclesiastical,* either because they originated in Church circles or because they concern Church matters, or because they are in some way under Church influence. However, very frequently the Church, as such, has nothing at all to do

with them and is in no way responsible for them; for instance, the prophecies of St. Malachy. We take them for what they are worth.

3 Some traditions are called *Apostolic,* because they originated with some one, or more, or with all, of the twelve Apostles, who, as rulers of the Church, thought it well to establish certain laws, customs or practices for the good of religion. For instance, the custom of keeping the seventh day holy, was transferred from Saturday to Sunday by Apostolic authority in commemoration of our Lord's resurrection from the dead, which took place on a Sunday. This is not a direct divine command; so the Church could change it again if she wished.

4 Some traditions are called *divine,* because they originated with God, *i. e.,* with Christ or the Holy Ghost. They came from God by a divine, supernatural revelation and are stamped with His authority. All the dogmas of the Christian religion were thus revealed and were originally promulgated by oral preaching, by Christ and His Apostles, many years before they were ever written down in the Books of the New Testament.

To make these important distinctions still more clearly understood, especially to those who have not as yet studied theology, let us explain them also *negatively* and show what they are not, as follows: —

1. Divine tradition, on which the Church depends, and professes to depend, for all her articles of faith, *is not the mere word of man.* For the word of man can never serve as the ground or motive for making

an act of divine faith, but, at most, only an act of human faith, which may easily deceive. As is well known, an act of divine faith depends on the authority of God, who must, therefore, reveal the truth to be thus believed

2. Divine tradition *is not the mere word of the Church.* The Church has authority to regulate discipline and to define the dogmas that were revealed in the beginning. But she does not pretend to receive new revelations; she does not originate new doctrines; unless the truths, or the doctrines proposed to our belief, were originally revealed to her through the Apostles in the beginning.

3. Divine tradition *is not the mere word of the Apostles.* It may have passed through them as its *channel,* but it did not originate with them as its *source,* it originated higher up, *i. e.,* with Christ or the Holy Ghost. St. Paul says that his word was not the word of men, but the very word of God "You received [the word] not as the word of men, but (as it is indeed) the word of God" (I Thess. 2, 13). The Apostles were not sent to teach their own ideas, but to teach what Christ had revealed to them and what He had commanded them to hand down to their immediate, legitimate successors, and they to others, and so all along down the line. "The things which thou hast heard from me in the presence of many witnesses, the same do thou transmit to faithful men who shall be able to teach others also" (II Tim. 2, 2).

Therefore, divine tradition is not the mere word of man; it is not the mere word of the Church; it is not

# CATHOLIC DOCTRINE OF TRADITION

the mere word of the Apostles; it is the word of God, the *infallible word* of the *infallible God*. Thus, the divine traditions on which the Church depends for her doctrines of faith and morals, have nothing whatever to do with the traditions or commandments of man, as Protestants so often pretend; they are also very different both from Apostolic and from ecclesiastical traditions. They are not the word of any man nor of any body of men; they are the word of Jesus Christ our Lord, who taught them by word of mouth to His Apostles in the beginning and through them to all ages, to the end of the world.

a) Divine and Apostolic traditions generally refer to matters of *faith and morals* only, such as the Blessed Trinity, the Incarnation, the inspiration and the divine authority of Sacred Scripture.

b) Ecclesiastical and human traditions usually refer to things of *lesser moment,* such as discipline, customs, practices, mere human historical facts, such as the date of composition, the integrity of the text and the human authorship, etc., of the Sacred Books.

## Divine-Ecclesiastical Traditions

In precise language, we often speak of " *divine-ecclesiastical traditions."* They are called " divine " because they originated with God; they are called " ecclesiastical " because they were not given, in the first instance, to private individuals and then left to their fate, to survive or perish; but they were entrusted to the Church and are safely transmitted by her, under the guidance of the Holy Ghost, to the end of time.

Of such Traditions God is the source. The Church is the channel.

If doctrines come down to us, not through Sacred Scripture, but through oral divine tradition, we should have for them the *same respect* and *reverence,* and we should feel precisely the same obligation to accept and to believe them, just as if they had reached us through the writings of the New Testament. For the value of a doctrine does not depend on the *channel* through which it reaches us. Its value depends on its *origin,* depends on the *source* from which it springs; depends on the *person* who first taught it and who made himself responsible for it. Now, in our case, the source, the origin of divine tradition is the person of our Lord Jesus Christ.

The Council of Trent has explained very clearly the nature and the value of divine tradition, where it declares that "the truths of the Gospel are contained in written books and in unwritten traditions, which [latter] were received by the Apostles from the lips of Christ Himself and were delivered, as it were, from hand to hand, and so have come down to us. Therefore we reverence with equal honor both the divine Scriptures and these divine traditions, which have been orally taught by Christ or by the Holy Ghost, and have been preserved in the Catholic Church by perpetual succession."[1]

All the truths of revealed religion are still taught in this self-same way by oral tradition; though, in the course of time, some of them have also been written

[1] Decree "*Sacrosancta,*" 4th session.

down in the New Testament Books under inspiration, and some of them have been written down in the works of the Fathers who were not inspired, but who were infallible collectively; and some have been written down in the doctrinal decrees of popes and councils and are infallible, even singly. But, though thus written, they are still called traditions and even *oral tradition,* because not written in inspired Scripture.

That some of the truths revealed by Christ were handed down in inspired writings and that the same and some other truths, also revealed by Him, were handed down orally, as He Himself had handed them down, was a merely *accidental* circumstance of little or no importance to any one. Both came from God and are equally true. Both were delivered to and through the Apostles and have the same divine authority. Both are the one word of God. Thus, it is not the mere fact of writing it down in a book with pen, ink, and paper that makes a thing to be or to become the word of God; but the fact that it was revealed or spoken by God, that is what makes it to be the word of God. For instance, the divinity of Christ was known and believed decades before it was written down in the New Testament. Therefore, it is not the writing that makes things true; the writing is merely one way of transmitting them and of making us know that they are true. They were true before they were written down.

## Mutual Relations Between Divine-Ecclesiastical Tradition and S. Scripture

It is important to understand some of the more essential mutual relations existing between divine-ecclesiastical tradition and Sacred Scripture, as follows:

1. Divine-ecclesiastical tradition is *prior in time* to the New Testament. It existed some decades before the New Testament was written. It has been in constant use ever since the first Pentecost Sunday, when the Church was first instituted; and there is no evidence to show that it ever underwent any change. It is in possession and can never be displaced by any human contrivance. This priority of tradition to Scripture is so manifest and so well established by the history of the early Church that it cannot be denied by any man who has a reputation to lose.

2. Divine-ecclesiastical tradition is *prior* to the New Testament, not only in the chronological, but also in the *logical order*. It is simply impossible to imagine Sacred Scripture as inspired and thus possessing divine authority, without first thinking of divine tradition, which is the only means of proving that Scripture *is* inspired. For, after all, the inspiration of the Bible can not be and must not be, gratuitously and ignorantly taken for granted. The inspiration of the Bible can no more be taken for granted than can the inspiration of the Rig Vedas, the Koran, or the Book of Mormon. Its inspiration can be and must be proved by rigorously valid arguments; that is, by arguments valid in proportion to the importance of the subject.

To believe in the inspiration of the Bible without valid arguments and without sufficient reasons for believing it, is not evidence of faith, but of superstition, much like the superstition of the Mohammedan, the Hindoo, or the Mormon. As we have already seen, all imaginable kinds of arguments have been tried, and the result of it all is this. No valid argument, no sufficient reason, has ever been advanced or ever can be advanced to prove the inspiration and divine authority of the Bible, unless it is based on the divine tradition of the Catholic Church; but, based on that tradition, the proof is most conclusive. No man ever thought or ever spoke more to the point on this subject than the great Augustine, when he wrote: " I would not believe the gospels, unless on the authority of the Catholic Church."

But does not the New Testament prove the inspiration of the New Testament and of the entire Bible? We reply: No Book of the New Testament claims to be divinely inspired; no Book of the New Testament claims to have God for its author and thus to possess divine authority; still less does any book of the New Testament make such claim for the entire collection of New Testament writings, nor even for any one book of the New Testament in such a way as to enable us to make an act of divine faith on the claim. St Peter, it is true, seems to claim inspiration for some of St Paul's Epistles, but we should remember that, at this stage of the proceedings, the inspiration and authority of St. Peter is as much in doubt as is the inspiration of St. Paul, and has to be proved before being used for such a purpose. Besides, II Peter is one of the seven deutero-canonical books of the New Testament and, for a long time, it was not generally accepted as canonical by the early Church and is still rejected by many Protestant scholars, so it can not be quoted consistently by Protestants for such a purpose. In any case, this book does not adequately prove the inspiration of any of Paul's Epistles, especially those that were not yet written at that time, and still less the inspiration of all the other books of the Bible.

3. Divine Tradition is wider *in scope* and more ample and comprehensive in its *contents* than Scripture. The Bible contains little or nothing but what was already found in tradition; whereas divine tradition contains many things taught by Christ and His Apostles, but which are not found in Scripture and which, nevertheless, have been accepted, not only by all Catholics, but also by Protestants of all denominations, as a necessary and integral part of their religion. Let us examine some of these strange cases:

a) The Catholic doctrine of the necessity and validity of "*infant baptism,*" which is clearly taught by divine tradition, has been adopted and practiced by an overwhelming majority of Protestants from the beginning of the "Reformation," though it is nowhere taught in the Bible nor is there any distinct trace of its practice to be found in the Good Book. Yet, it is positively taught by Catholic tradition and, therefore, Protestants, by admitting it, contradict very clearly their own rule of "the Bible and nothing but the Bible, as a guide to religion."

b) The practice of *"washing one another's feet"* must seem, to any one but a Catholic, to be most strictly commanded in the Bible and to be a definitely established institution among Christians. (John 13, 1-17.) Yet it has never been so regarded by the Catholic Church; for the words of Our Lord in this passage seem to express no more than a willingness, on the part of good Christians, to do for one another *any* act of kindness, however servile or humiliating it may be. In this case, therefore, Protestants, who practice this rite as little as Catholics do, abandon their own fundamental rule of the sufficiency of the Bible in matters of religion and follow Catholic tradition.

c) In the law of Moses the Hebrews were forbidden *"to eat blood,"* and even yet this law is observed by Jews. (Levit 7, 26.) Also, at the first Council of Jerusalem, the Apostles approved this same law and very explicitly imposed it upon all Christian converts, whether of Jewish or of Gentile origin. (Acts 15, 20-29.) Though this precept is so clearly taught in the Bible, still Protestants neglect it, because they are assured solely by the uniform tradition of the Catholic Church that that law was never intended to be of permanent obligation.

d) In the Sermon on the Mount we are distinctly commanded *"not to swear at all."* (Matt. 5, 34.) But Protestants, without any authorization from the text, do not consider this precept as binding and thus abandon their own fundamental rule of the sufficiency of the Bible alone as a guide to religion, and follow the Catholic rule.

e) Nothing is more clearly or more emphatically insisted upon in the Bible than the precept of "*keeping holy the Sabbath Day*," as prescribed in Gen. 2, 2–3; Exod. 16, 23; 26, 25–30; 20, 8–11. "The seventh day is the Sabbath of the Lord." Of course, all but the most ignorant know that the Biblical Sabbath is Saturday and not Sunday; know that it is the seventh or last day and not the first day of the week. They also know that Christ observed the Sabbath on the seventh day (Luke 4, 16, 23, 56 and 66), and that the Jews still observe this law in spite of Christian usage to the contrary. And yet Protestants, by neglecting it, inconsistently contradict their own rule of belief and practice and adopt the Catholic rule of tradition. Thus with all their repugnance to tradition and to the Catholic Church, Protestants have found themselves absolutely obliged, in many instances, to admit them both. As we have just seen, they are obliged to admit tradition in order to prove that Scripture is Scripture; for without admitting tradition to prove Scripture, they can neither know that there are any writings at all that are inspired, nor which, in particular, these writings are, nor what versions or translations, or publications of them are genuine.

"To understand its place in the life of the Church, we should know that tradition is a fixed body of definite truth, scattered through the works of the Fathers and the publications of councils, dealing with fixed doctrines and definite statements and these are as continuous and unchangeable as the doctrines directly contained in Scripture, though subject, like them and all other knowledge, to a continuous development of expression on the part of the '*Ecclesia docens*' and of apprehension on the part of the '*Ecclesia discens.*' . . . Tradition, then, is not a fluctuating body of opinions; it is a *fixed* standard. It is not only the dogmatic interpretation of Scripture, but it is also a *positive* body of *definite* truth contained in itself It is the entire revelation of Christianity. It is the whole message committed to the Church by Our Lord, while Scripture is but a collection of inspired books, whose only guarantee is tradition Scripture is a part of tradition, rather than tradition an appendix to Scripture. . . . The Church does not consist of a series of generations sharply separated by centuries or movements, but she is a kind of permanent person, who lives continuously through the ages, remembering the revelation once made to her, and incessantly stating and re-stating it. Tradition, then, roughly speaking, is her *memory* of that revelation, and of the events that heralded it and followed it; it is her recollection of the deductions drawn from it. . . . Tradition, in a real sense, is a continuous memory of the whole gospel. Tradition transcends traditions just as education in general transcends particular lessons or just as a musician's knowledge of music exceeds the sum of the pieces which he composes and performs." (R. H. Benson, *Infallibility and Tradition*, pp 1 to 9.)

DIVINE TRADITION HAS COME DOWN TO US

1) In professions of faith and definitions of councils.
2) In the sacred liturgy — ceremonies, etc.

3) In the acts of the holy martyrs.
4) In the writings of the holy Fathers.
5) In ecclesiastical history.
6) In the catacombs, especially Roman.
7) In the sacred monuments, churches, images, etc. " The stones will cry out " (Luc. 19, 40).

### The Catholic Doctrine of Tradition

Having, sufficiently for our purpose, explained the meaning of tradition in general, and some of its many varieties, we may now venture to lay down the following.

### Proposition

*Divine Tradition, as interpreted by the Catholic Church, is a most reliable source of revealed religion and, even more than Scripture itself, is an essential part of the Catholic rule of faith and of the Catholic principle of hermeneutics.*

This proposition may be proved in many ways, especially

1. By the clearest statement of Scripture itself;
2. By the unanimous testimony of the early Fathers;
3. By the history of the Church in Apostolic times.

### 1. *The Teaching of Scripture*

I. This proposition is proved beyond cavil by Scripture itself, which teaches, in just so many words, the existence of another concurrent and parallel channel of revelation along with Scripture and which clearly shows that the unwritten word of God was already in existence and was in full force and general operation long before the New Testament was ever composed. In other words, in many passages of the New Testament we are referred to oral divine tradition as to a clearer, more complete and previously existing channel of revealed truth.

The New Testament writers either (a) expressly pre-supposed in their Christian reader a previously acquired and more complete knowledge of Christian doctrine (received from oral tradition) than what they propose to teach in their Epistles and other writings; or, (b) they refer the reader to some subsequent oral instruction to be given to him later by the regular pastors of the Church. Of this the following examples are too clear to need explanation.

St. Paul says: " Therefore, brethren, stand firm and hold the traditions which you have been taught, whether by word [of mouth] or by our Epistle " (II Thess 2, 14) Here the Apostle commands us to receive both the written and the unwritten word of God and to receive them with equal reverence and obedience.

Again he says: " The things which thou hast heard from me before many witnesses, the same commit [not to writing, but] to faithful men, who shall be able to teach others also " (II Tim. 2, 2).

Again he says: " Hold the form of sound words which thou hast heard from me in faith " (II Tim. 1, 13).

St. John writes: " Beloved, I write no new commandment to you, but an old commandment, which you had from the beginning; the old commandment is the word which you have heard" (I John 2, 7).

Again he says: "I have not written to you, as if you did not know the truth, but because you know it [the truth]. Let that abide in you which you heard from the beginning" (I John 5, 20–21).

Again: "I have many things to write to you, Gaius, but I am unwilling to write them to you with pen and ink, but I hope shortly to see you and we shall speak face to face" (III John 13–14)

The presence of the verb "heard" and the absence of the verb read in these passages show that the Apostle is speaking of oral tradition, and not of written instructions

From these same passages it is also evident that the New Testament writers wished what they wrote to be understood either in the light of what they had already taught by oral tradition or according to what they were afterwards to teach orally or "face to face." Even today the same relationship exists between Sacred Scripture and divine tradition, or between the written and the spoken word, as existed in the days of the Apostles. Therefore, the Catholic interpreter must follow divine tradition. The words of Christ in conferring this mission upon His Apostles, refer clearly, not to the written word, which did not yet exist, but only to the spoken word, to oral preaching. The conclusion is that since we should accept everything that is taught in Scripture, we should accept divine tradition also, as of equal authority with Scripture; for so the Scripture commands us to do.

## 2. The Teaching of the Fathers

II Our proposition is proved also by the unanimous consent of the Fathers, of whom we shall cite only a few for the sake of brevity.

St. *Ignatius Martyr*, Bishop of Antioch (A. D. 107), was a disciple of the Apostles. On his way to Rome, to be devoured by the wild beasts in the amphitheatre, he said to the Christians who visited him, " Hold firmly the traditions of the Apostles." (Eusebius, *Church History*, Book 3, Chap. 30.)

St. *Irenaeus*, writing about A. D. 180, says " Nothing is more easy for those who seek the truth than to observe the traditions which the Apostles have left to all the world . . . the pastors of the Church have received the inheritance of the truth . . . the tongues of nations vary, but tradition is everywhere one and the same." " Supposing the Apostles had not left us the Scriptures, ought we not still to have followed the traditions which they consigned to those to whom they committed the Church? It is this rule of tradition which many nations of barbarians, believing in Christ, follow without the use of letters or ink." (*Against Heresies*, Book 1, 3; 3, 2; 3, 5; 4, 23; 4, 64).

St. *Basil*, writing towards the end of the fourth century, says. " There are many doctrines preserved and preached in the Church which are derived partly from written documents and partly from Apostolic tradition, which have equally the same force in religion and which no one contradicts who has the least knowledge of the Christian laws " (*On the Holy Spirit*).

St. *Epiphanius*, in the beginning of the fifth century, says: "We must make use of tradition; for all things are not to be found in Sacred Scripture" (*On Heresies*, 61).

St. John *Chrysostom*, writing about the year 400, says: "Hence it is plain that the Apostles did not deliver to us everything by their Epistles, but many things without writing. These are equally worthy of belief. Hence, let us regard the tradition of the Church as the subject of our belief. Such and such a thing is a tradition; seek no further."

St. *Augustine*, also writing about the year 400, says: "There are many things observed by the universal Church, which are justly held to have been appointed by the Apostles, though they are not written" (*De Baptismo*).

St. *Vincent of Lerins*, about 450, says: "You are to interpret the divine text according to the tradition of the Catholic Church." He then says: "What has been believed in all places, at all times, and by all the faithful ("*quod semper, quod ubique, quod ab omnibus*"), must have been derived from divine and Apostolic tradition." (*Commonitorium*.)

This is the unanimous opinion of all the Fathers. For a more ample collection of the testimony of the early Fathers, the student may consult Milner's *End of Controversy*, Letter X; also Tanquerey, *Theol. Dogmat. Fundam.*, pp. 625 ff.

### 3. *The Teaching of Church History*

III. Our proposition is proved in a still more remarkable manner also by the history of the Church in Apostolic times, where the student will find some very interesting and important facts bearing on the subject.

It is certain that Christ and His Apostles promulgated all the revealed doctrines of the Christian religion in the beginning, not in writing, but by word of mouth, by oral divine tradition. This is evident from the following facts and considerations. —

In the gospels we read that Our Blessed Lord, by His charming personality and by the persuasiveness of His manner, and by His gentle yet irresistible eloquence, drew around Him great multitudes of followers.

From among these followers He chose seventy-two to be, in a special manner, His disciples. From among these seventy-two disciples He chose twelve to be in a more special manner, His Apostles.

From among these twelve Apostles He chose one, Peter, to be, in a most special manner, their chief and His vicar on earth.

And of these Apostles and disciples, and of the faithful under them, He formed His Church and made it subject to Himself, as its sovereign head.

And to this Church, and especially to the Apostles and their successors, He entrusted, for safe keeping, all the truths which He had come to reveal to the world, truths of which He said: " For this was I born and for this came I into the world to give testimony to the truth "

He commanded His Apostles to preach those truths to all nations to the end of time, and sent them to confound the learned philosophers of Greece and of Rome and to plant Christianity on the ruins of paganism throughout the world.

To enable them to perform properly this superhuman task, He, on two memorable occasions, promised them His assistance in words of solemn import,— words which explain most abundantly the whole Catholic position on this subject, and which should never be forgotten.

1. The *first promise* was made in His farewell discourse, just after the *Last Supper,* when He said to His chosen twelve: "The Paraclete, the spirit of truth, whom the Father will send in my name, He will teach you all things, and bring to your minds all things, whatsoever I have said to you" (John 14, 26).

2. The *second promise* was made on the *mountain in Galilee,* before His ascension into Heaven, when Our Lord said to the twelve: "He that heareth you, heareth me; as the Father hath sent me, so I also send you. All power is given to me in Heaven and on earth, Go ye, therefore, into the whole world. Teach all nations; preach the Gospel to every creature, and behold, I am with you all days, even to the end of the world" (Matt. 28, 19–20; Luke 10, 16 *et al.*).

The words of the first promise clearly mean that the *Holy Spirit of God* dwells permanently in the Church and abides with her forever; that He fills her with the gift of holiness and sanctifies her children to the end of time; and especially that He teaches her all truth without error and brings to her remembrance all things whatsoever Our Lord Jesus Christ hath said to her.

The words of the second promise mean that *Our Lord Jesus Christ* Himself is also with His Church and will be with her to the end, to guide her, to protect her, and to direct her in all that is necessary to fulfill her mission of saving the world, and, especially, He is with her to prevent her from teaching any errors. The words, " He that heareth you, heareth me; as the Father sent me, so I also send you; the Holy Ghost will teach you all truth, and will bring to your remembrance all things whatsoever I have said to you; and behold, I am with you all days,"— these words show the perfect identity of the teachings of the Church with the teachings of Our Lord Jesus Christ,— show that He has transferred to her His authority, as far as needed;— show that He has made her His representative, to continue His work on earth; and that, for His honor's sake, He will see to it that she represents Him faithfully.

This promise of the future presence of both the Holy Ghost and of our Blessed Lord in the Church was *explicit* and *absolute,* and *without any limitation or restriction of time, place, person, or truth.*

Most readers probably have noticed the universality of these final instructions of Our Lord to His Apostles, expressed by the words, " *each,*" " *every,*" " *all,*" " *whole.*" It is this universality of His language and thought that makes the Church Catholic, which means universal, for He says: "Go ye into the *whole* world; teach *all* nations; preach the Gospel to *every* creature; the Holy Ghost will teach you *all* things, and will bring to your minds *all* things *whatsoever* I have said to you; and behold, I am with you *all* days." And then, as if not content with these words of unlimited meaning, he gives, if possible, still greater emphasis to the promise by saying, "Behold, I am with you all days, *even to the end of the world."*

It is in consequence of this *permanent in-dwelling* of the Holy Spirit of God, it is in consequence of this *active presence* of Our Lord Jesus Christ in her, that the Church is made one, holy, Catholic, Apostolic, indestructible, unchangeable, everlasting, and infallible,— that is, endowed with the gift of teaching *all truth, all days, to all men, in all places* and without the possibility of teaching error.

In consequence of this indwelling of the Spirit of God in her, the Church, from the very beginning, from the first Pentecost Sunday, was already full-fledged and fully organized in everything essential to her existence and future work; she possessed, (1) the entire body of revealed truth; she was furnished with (2) a hierarchical order consisting of Apostles and their legitimate successors in office, the bishops and priests of the Church; she already had (3) her sacramental system for conferring grace and for sanctifying her people, and, with the words of Christ, as above quoted, continually ringing in her ears to remind her of her duty to God and to man, and conscious that she was thoroughly organized and fully equipped for her work, the Church was already actively and zealously engaged in her mission of Christianizing and civilizing the nations throughout the entire Greco-Roman Empire as well as instructing numerous barbarian tribes living beyond the limits of civilization, for perhaps twenty years before the first book of the New Testament was written; and for more than sixty years before the last book of the New Testament was written; and for 300 years before the collection or catalogue of the New Testament Books was known or was practically available to one out of ten thousand of the people; and for 1400 years before the invention of printing, after which Holy Scripture became generally available for the first time, but without ever becoming the normal, practical rule of faith to Christians.

As should be remembered, the *first* New Testament Book to be written was either St. Matthew's Gospel or, more probably, the Epistle to the Galatians, or that to the Thessalonians, which was not composed for about twenty years after the Ascension of Christ

The *last* book of the New Testament to be written was St. John's Gospel, which was composed between 60 and 65 years after the Ascension.

The other Gospels and the Epistles were written between these two dates, that is, between twenty and sixty years after the Resurrection of Christ.

But even after the New Testament was *completed,* it was practically inaccessible, and practically useless, even as a partial rule of faith and conduct, to the great majority of Christians for many centuries. For, in the early ages, the New Testament books were known and circulated chiefly in those particular parts of the Church (city, province, nation) to which they were originally addressed, such as the Epistles to the Romans, to the Corinthians, to the Ephesians. For 200 or 300 years, entire *collections* of all the New Testament books could be found nowhere except, perhaps, in some of the larger Christian centres or communities, such as Rome, Alexandria, Antioch. Then, too, in many parts of the Church, the New Testament books were not easily distinguishable from the extensive *apocryphal* literature of the times, such as false gospels, false epistles falsely ascribed to holy and reputable men as their authors, though in reality written by heretics for the purpose of deceiving the simple and unwary. The process of separating and sifting out the Sacred Books from the profane or spurious literature of those days was necessarily so very slow and so gradual, that the New Testament books were not collected into a volume, apart by themselves, for generations, for 200 or 300 years, neither were they put upon the canon or the official catalogue of Scriptural Books in such a public and authoritative way as to remove all doubt or uncertainty from the minds of the faithful about the character and value of the books nor in such a way as to make them of practical use to Christians, as guides in religion,— until the close of the fourth century.

This was done completely and for the first time under Pope Damasus I, in a council held at Rome, *A. D. 383,* in a decree entitled, " What the Universal Catholic Church holds and what it forbids," in regard to Holy Scripture. It was done for the second time at the

CATHOLIC DOCTRINE OF TRADITION 145

Council of Hippo, *A. D. 393,* and again in the Third Council of Carthage, *A. D. 397.*

Until this was done publicly and officially, few Christians *could* know for certain, which books were inspired and authoritative, and which were not inspired and not authoritative; and consequently many would read none of them.

And still fewer people thought much or cared much about the matter, for, in those days not one Christian, perhaps, in a thousand could read; and, even if they could read, not one perhaps in ten thousand could get much, if any, meaning out of those books, even if he were rich enough to own a copy.

In fact, we may say, that the most glorious period in the history of the Christian Church had already passed away, before the books of the New Testament were known (except, perhaps, in name) to the great bulk of Christians; and hundreds of thousands of Christians, many of them saints and martyrs, had already lived and *died in holiness* without ever having seen a book (or, at most, only some stray book) of the New Testament; and without being able to read even that, and still less able to understand it properly, or to buy a copy, so rare and so costly were such books in those early days.

This is all the more manifest when we consider that the New Testament was written in *Greek* and was unintelligible to vast multitudes of Christians for some centuries after Christ. For great numbers of Christians understood neither Greek, nor Latin, nor Syriac " In fact, it was only after the doctrines of the Christian religion had been everywhere preached, accepted, practiced, defined in creeds, embodied in Sacraments, symbolized in ceremonies, typified in divine public worship, and thus engraved, as it were, on the memory of the universal Church under the influence of the Spirit of God, that the books of the New Testament were written." (Card. Manning.) And it is well to bear in mind that the books of the New Testament were written, not to unbelievers, not to Jews or Pagans, but to believers, to Christian individuals or communities; to those who already had the faith and were baptized. It is well to bear in mind that these books always recognize in those to whom they are addressed, a *previous knowledge* of the truths of the faith; they always take for granted, they presuppose, in their readers, an intimate acquaintance with the Christian religion, which had been taught to them, in some cases, by the writer himself, or by some other Apostle, or Apostolic man,— taught to them, as is often expressly stated in the context, by word of mouth, by oral preaching, years before the first book of the New Testament was written.

Yet during this long period the Church had spread from the Pillars of Hercules in the West, to India and China in the far East; and from the savage tribes in the frozen North, to the desert sands of Egypt and Arabia in the distant South. During this long period, also, the gates of the Heavenly Jerusalem stood wide ajar to admit the legions of Christian men and women who had died in the odor of sanctity, including thousands of martyrs who, in unspeakable torments, had

CATHOLIC DOCTRINE OF TRADITION 147

shed their blood for Him who had died for them. During this long period millions of people became Christians in various lands, and believed the whole truth of the Church, as we believe it now, and became saints before they ever saw, read, or heard a single word of the New Testament, for the very simple reason that *the New Testament did not yet exist.* How, then, did they become Christians? In the same way that pagans and others become Christians today,— by hearing the truth preached by the pastors of the Church. " Faith cometh by hearing."

Certainly no man will die for a false religion, at least, not if he knows it is false, nor even for the true religion, unless he knows for certain that it is the true religion, and unless it is authenticated by evidence that demands assent and that compels obedience.

But on account of their nearness, both in time and in place, to the cradle of Christianity, the early Christians were in a position to obtain the strongest evidence to the claims of the Church on their conscience and to their obedience, and no one will deny that *they* were true Christians.

So we ask· What was it that brought those early Christians out of Judaism or out of paganism into the bosom of the Christian Church? What was the motive that led so many of them to face death joyfully for the love of Jesus Christ? What was the ground on which they built their expectations of life everlasting beyond the skies? In other words, What was their rule of faith?

It certainly was not a cold, lifeless book, which few

of them had ever seen or even heard of. It was not even the books of the New Testament, which are so beautiful, so sublime, so profound, so full of the sentiments of faith and hope and love, and of the choicest virtues inculcated by the Christian religion.

What, then, was the rule of faith of those early Christians? It was the Catholic rule of faith None other was possible. No book of the New Testament was yet in existence. Their rule was the living voice of the Catholic Church, to which Christ Our Lord had given authority to teach in His name, and to teach unerringly whatsoever he had told her to teach to the end of time. It was the manifest claims of the Catholic Church, to whose keeping He had entrusted all his divine teachings and all the other means of salvation which He had established forever. He had appointed His Church to be the guardian and interpreter of the *whole word of God,* both written and unwritten, and He had clothed her with a beauty and a majesty and a holiness that made her her own witness. " She walks a queen " (*Procedit Regina*).

Without doubt, what the Church, without the written Word, did so successfully for twenty, sixty, and even for hundreds of years, she, assisted by the same indwelling Spirit of God, could continue to do forever. In such a case what has been done once or what can be done at all, can be done forever.

As the original revelation had existed many years without any part of it being written down, so, too, it existed and continued to flourish 1400 years before printing was invented; and, if pen, ink, and paper and the printing press had never been used to perpetuate and propagate it, still its doctrines would have survived all the same and would have retained all their original purity and completeness.

From our Lord's words quoted by Matthew 28, 18-20; Luke 10, 16; and John 14, 26, we necessarily conclude that it was the will and the intention of Our Lord that His religion should be established, maintained, and extended progressively down through the ages, to the end of time, chiefly and primarily and normally by instruction given by word of mouth, by explaining verbally the truths contained in divine tradition, by oral preaching delivered by the legitimate pastors of the Church, just as it continues to be done today in the Catholic Church

Our Lord Himself always preached by word of mouth and commanded His Apostles to do the same. He never wrote anything and never commanded His Apostles to write anything; neither, of course, did He forbid them to write. It was a matter of practical indifference whether they wrote or not. For, even if they wrote, it could not change the already established order of things. They committed their doctrines [not to writing, but] to faithful men, who should be able to teach others also (II Tim. 2, 2).

Besides, if Our Lord had intended that all men should learn His religion from a book, from the New Testament, there can be no doubt that He Himself would have written that book and would have imposed upon all men the obligation of learning to read it, and, since He never commands what is impossible, He should and would have furnished all men with the means of obtaining and of reading and of understanding that book properly. Yet He never did anything of the sort Had He done so, it would have been a fundamental precept of His religion to learn to read, in order to read that one book, whereas we know for certain that He never wrote anything Himself, never commanded His Apostles to write anything, and never commanded His people to learn to read anything. And even after the New Testament was written, He did not impose it on men as the sole means of learning His religion. If that were the case, then, in order to become a Christian, the first thing necessary would be to learn the alphabet. Yet, taking all ages and all climes from His time down to the end of the world and striking a general average, He must have known that not one in a hundred Christians would be able to read at all and not one in a thousand would be able to read and properly understand one solitary page of the Bible.

Had Our Lord commanded His Apostles to write, they would all have obeyed, they would all have written. Yet the majority of them (seven in number) never wrote anything, and those that did write either wrote so little, or wrote in such a way as to show very clearly that they did not consider it an essential part of their duty to write at all. They show that it never was their intention to commit to writing the whole truth which they had been preaching by word of mouth, but only such snatches or portions of it as incidentally served their purpose and sufficed to answer the questions proposed to them This is clear from the character and the scope of the New Testament. From this we conclude that, were it not for those circumstances and had the occasion not presented itself, the New Testament books might never have been written. For those writings are not an essential part of the Christian system. They are occasional in purpose. They are partial and incomplete in compass. They are jerky in style and disjointed in method. They are mostly local in interest and fragmentary in character. They really are just what we might expect them to be under the circumstances of those times, places and persons.

Written on such different occasions and on such disconnected topics, the most natural consequence of it all is that in those writings there is nothing to show that any one of them, or all of them put together, contain, or were ever intended to contain, an orderly, clear, detailed treatise or systematic exposition or well rounded out explanation of any one doctrine or precept of the Christian religion, still less of the entire collection of the teachings of faith and morals.

Evidently, then, the thought furthest from the mind of the New Testament writers was that their occasional letters, which are so incomplete and desultory, and which were cast off, apparently, in any which way and on the spur of the moment, should ever be gathered into a volume and made to do enforced duty, as a complete and all-sufficient exposition of belief and conduct.

In the opinion of the Apostles, oral preaching by the pastors of the Church was the natural, normal and only practical method of teaching the people; it was the method established by Christ Himself both by precept and by His own example.

From all this it clearly follows that, even after the New Testament had been written, the already-existing divine tradition, and the already-established authority of the Church as interpreter of tradition and of Scripture, were not in any way diminished or replaced by the written Word in the New Testament. Consequently, the unwritten Word, or divine tradition, is still in force as an integral and essential part of the Catholic principle of interpretation.

Accordingly, in obedience to the command and in imitation of the example of Christ, the Apostles all spent their lives preaching by word of mouth, in one direction, from Judea to Spain and, in another direction, from Judea to India, everywhere founding churches and "commending their doctrine to faithful men who should be able to teach others also" (II Tim 2, 2). And "these faithful men who were able to teach others also," were the legitimate successors of the Apostles, and their authority to teach is a fundamental element in the constitution of the Church. Inspired writings are something added on, over and above, by a special providence of God, but, while such writings are very useful, still they are not strictly essential. The Church can get along without them. The proof of this is that she did get along without them entirely for years, and, practically, for centuries.

## Protestant Objections Refuted

Nearly all Protestants admit that "the Bible, the whole Bible and nothing but the Bible, as interpreted by private judgment, is the Protestant rule of faith and morals." Accordingly, they claim to accept, as a part of their faith, everything that is found in the Bible, and they pretend to reject, as not being a part of their faith, everything that is not found in the Bible. Both statements are false, as we can easily show.

Evidently, this rule is an essential part of their religion, just as much as the foundation of a house is an essential part of the house, which is built upon it and rests upon it. And yet, is it not strange, is it not passing strange, that this rule, which is such a necessary and essential part of their religion, is not found in the Bible? The plain fact is that there is not so much as one single text in the entire range of the Bible, from Genesis to the Apocalypse, that asserts, either implicitly or explicitly, that either "the Bible" alone, whether in whole or in part, or the Bible as interpreted by mere human reason in any of its many forms, is the Christian's rule or anybody's rule of faith and morals.

Therefore, the Catholic rule is still in possession; for there was never a time when it was not recognized and practiced. If any one questions this fact, we may ask him when, where, how, why and by what authority was the original Catholic rule abolished and this modern Protestant rule substituted instead? To legalize their rule, Protestants should do these three things:

1. They should show, by solid arguments, that at

some time and at what time, in the last 1800 years, the ancient Catholic rule was abolished;

2. They should show that precisely *this* Protestant rule and not any other rule was substituted in its place;

3. They should show that all this was done, not by unauthorized Protestant reformers in the sixteenth century, A. D., but by the authority of Our Lord Jesus Christ, who alone, in such matters, has the fullest right to do and to undo, as He chooses.

Yet they have proved nothing of the sort. For, to prove all this, it would require a new revelation from Heaven, which has never been given, nor has any remotest trace of it ever been found The Protestant principle, therefore, is ruled out as a novelty, and as an innovation too modern to deserve attention.

*The Place of S. Scripture in the Church*

Many of those who differ from us in other respects are forced, by the very nature of the case, to admit that the Church was perfect in her constitution and fully equipped with all essentially belonging to her from the first Pentecost day. This is the same as to admit that the New Testament books are not an essential part of her framework; since no book of the New Testament existed at all at that early date, nor for many years afterwards. Therefore, in the teaching department of the Church these writings continue to hold a place *relatively subordinate* to the Church, and coordinate with the unwritten Word or divine tradition, of which they are only a duplicate part They hold the place which the Church, guided by the Holy Ghost, who inspired them, assigned to them, and she still retains the right to determine how they are to be interpreted and how far, in given circumstances, they are to be used by the people.

It is evident, therefore, that the Holy Scriptures hold only a subordinate, and not an essential, place in the teaching department of the Church. They are only a collateral and coordinate element in the plan of her constitution. The Spirit of Christ, by His energizing presence in the Church, makes her infallible for the purpose of teaching his whole revelation officially and unerringly. From this it follows, that everything that serves as a vehicle or as an instrument of that teaching, whether written or oral, or in any other form, must be subordinate, in a sense, to her control. Sacred Scripture is, therefore, on a level with Divine Tradition.

If that were not so, it would follow that the dead letter, say, of one of St. Paul's Epistles, would have more weight and more authority than the living word of Paul himself, though he were actually present and able to explain his own words. We, therefore, infer that one of Paul's Epistles could not possess more authority than Paul himself, and could not, in any way, supplant him or nullify his oral teaching, or deprive him of the position of the authority which he had so long exercised as a teacher, before he wrote his Epistle. On the contrary, he would ever retain the right to explain the meaning of his own Epistles and to interpret them in accordance with the ever varying circumstances of the times; also the Church, of which he was a member, would inherit the same right of interpretation.

But, it may be asked, has not the New Testament, which contains a considerable portion of Christian revelation, a place in the plan of the Christian Church? A place, yes; but not an essential place. A place, yes; but a subordinate place, a place subordinate to the Church and coordinate with divine tradition, of which Scripture, after all, is only a part,— a part put down in writing. A moment's reflection will show how very reasonable this statement is.

By the words "essential" part or element we mean what is indispensable to a thing, we mean what belongs to the intrinsic nature of a thing; we mean what is absolutely necessary, and without which the thing could neither begin to exist nor continue to exist. This being the meaning of the word, we may say that the books of the New Testament are not an essential part of the Church; for the simple reason that the Church existed and flourished and did her work with marvelous success many years before the books of the New Testament were written.

We say that the New Testament books are useful to the Church; yes, they are of great assistance to her in facilitating her work; yes, certainly. But they are not necessary to the continuance of her life, nor so indispensable that, without them, she could not properly spread the Gospel of truth, nor propagate her influence to the good of humanity. Else Christ would have made them an essential part of her being from the outset, an essential element in her constitution from the very beginning, from the first Pentecost Sunday.

As already said, the Church was in existence many years before the New Testament was written. The Church, therefore, is not the effect or the result of the New Testament. It was not caused by the New Testament.

On the contrary, the Church produced the New Testament through certain members of her teaching corps, while engaged in her ministry of teaching. The New Testament, then, belongs to the Church. It is her property. It was entrusted to her for safe-keeping and for her future use, and it is her duty to explain it to her people.

God has made his Church the official depository, the careful guardian, and the authentic interpreter of the New Testament as of all revelation, whether oral or written, whether found in Scripture or in divine tradition, and has given her the right to impose her interpretations, in doctrinal matters, on all Chrisians, and, as such, she continues to explain its contents now, just as she explained them before they were even written down in the New Testament.

Thus, then, the Bible the property of the Catholic Church and as explained by the Catholic Church; yes, that is all right; that is as God intended it to be.

But the Bible alone; the Bible independent of the Church; the Bible without the Church; the Bible above the Church; the Bible against the Church; the Bible against that very Church which produced it and preserved it for long centuries, no; that is all wrong, all very absurd both in theory and in practice. The first is the Catholic, the second is the Protestant position.

The New Testament books were written years after the Church was established. Hence, they were introduced into a system *already fully equipped,* and permanently established, and furnished with all the means essentially necessary to do its work. They were introduced into an organism *already fully supplied* with all the members necessary to its complete development, according to the original ideal of its founder. The method of spreading the Gospel by oral teaching still remained in force in fact as from the beginning of the human race.

Therefore the books of the New Testament were never meant by Christ to supplant or to supersede, to suspend or to put aside or, in any way, to belittle the need of that oral teaching which Christ had commanded should be observed to the end of time. Nowhere in the New Testament is there the faintest intimation that such a substitution could ever be made.

In other words: the New Testament books were introduced into a system *complete in all its essentials.* They were introduced into a system *already cast in a mould* and *unalterably fixed* by a divine decree. In other words, the New Testament books appeared on the scene years and years later — from twenty to sixty years — too late in the day, to be more than coordinate with divine tradition, of which they are really only a part, a part committed to writing.

Instruction by word of mouth, or oral teaching by

the pastors of His Church, is the natural, normal, logical, divinely established method by which our Divine Lord, in imitation of his own example, wished to have the Gospel propagated and preserved among all the nations of the world, from the beginning to the end; and so He gave to his Church an authority and a fitness for teaching His truths, everywhere and always, and without admixture of error, down through the ages. He gave to her an authority of which she can never be deprived by any power under Heaven,— an authority which can never be either suspended or supplanted, which can never be either abrogated or annulled, which can never be either replaced or displaced, by any other contrivance, — an authority which she had from the very beginning, and which she shall have to the end; — an authority supreme, permanent, and perfectly equal to the task of spreading and preserving His doctrines independently of all other teaching agencies, such as printed records, even though such records be inspired in the fullest sense and in the highest degree.

It is clear that, while writing was of great assistance later on, yet it is not an essential means to the end. And the reason of it is that the Church was so constructed by her divine Founder that her authority to teach and her efficiency in teaching, and her uniform accuracy in teaching, and her unparalleled success in teaching, were not made to depend on the invention of the alphabet, nor on written documents, nor on costly manuscripts, nor on printed books, nor on the penmanship of any scribe, nor on the art of any writer, nor on the enterprise of any publisher, nor on any other modern contrivance, whether of a mechanical or electrical or what not nature.

Teaching by word of mouth is nature's own method. Still more, it is God's own method; for God is the author of nature. It is the only method of teaching used, or that could possibly have been used, from the days of Adam, through some thousands of years, to the invention of the alphabet. It is the only method used during the thousands of years that elapsed from the invention of the alphabet to the invention of the printing press. And it is the very nature of things that this method of teaching by oral tradition will continue to the end of the world. It is unavoidable; nothing can take its place.

These facts and considerations make it as clear as anything can be, that it never was the intention of Christ to substitute the New Testament instead of, and to the exclusion of, the authority of the Apostles and their successors, whom He had appointed to teach in His name, and with whom He had promised to remain all days, even to the end of the world.

It never was intended, and it never could have been intended, that Christians should turn a deaf ear to the living voice of the teaching body to whom Christ had given authority to teach in His name, and should fashion themselves a religion from the cold, lifeless pages of a book,— and that book, mind you, written by those self-same teachers. Nowhere in all the New Testament is there the faintest hint or intimation of such a substitution made or ever to be made.

A collection of books, such as the New Testament, the latest portion of which did not exist until the Church had already propagated her whole revelation by oral teaching throughout the nations for sixty years and more,— a collection of books which was not practically at hand nor practically available in its complete and final form for general use, until she had taught that revelation by word of mouth for more than three hundred years, and even for fourteen hundred years, could not take the place of, or supersede that method of oral teaching of which the Lord Himself had given both the example and precept, unless He Himself had explicitly declared that it should be so. Yet He never so declared.

The fact is that no religion was ever yet effectually planted and successfully propagated among men exclusively by means of a book, but only by instruction given by word of mouth and by example. The Christian religion, which is no exception to this rule, was not derived originally from the books of the New Testament. It does not depend on those books either for its first origin, for they were not yet written, or for its later continuance; either for its first introduction into the world or for its subsequent preservation and continuous propagation down through the ages.

If " the Bible, the whole Bible and nothing but the Bible " were placed in the hand of a man who had never lived in a Christian country, who *had never heard anything* about the Christian religion, and who was told to get his religion out of that book,— what *kind of a religion would it be?* We would be safe in saying that a religion thus formed would be a *mental* and *moral absurdity*, a *psychological* and *ontological* monstrosity, unlike anything " in the heavens above or on the earth beneath or in the waters under the earth." Which simply means that the Bible, to get the right sense out of it, must be interpreted according to the divine tradition of the Catholic Church.

All Catholics admit that divine and Apostolic and ecclesiastical traditions are valid sources of theological knowledge and of historical information, and are, therefore, valid sources of argument for proving both the human and the divine authority of Scripture. Human tradition is also a reliable source of historical information, when, as is often the case, the requisite conditions are verified.

### Tradition the First Rule of Christianity

All advanced critics and many Protestants reject tradition in general as entirely or nearly worthless, both for theological and for critical purposes. However, among Protestants, there are some distinguished exceptions.

1. One class of critics contend that tradition should always be admitted on principle and as a general preliminary condition to all discussions, and that it should ever and always be accepted as a reliable source of information, especially in higher criticism.

2. Another class of critics reject tradition as a general principle and antecedently to any investigation into, *e.g.*, the human authority of Scripture. They declare it entirely useless.

3. A third class of critics maintain that both these positions are uncritical and exaggerated.

1. As against the first class of extremists, we know that there are traditions and traditions; that some mere human traditions have never been traced back to any well known, reliable source, nor to a relatively high antiquity; that no one knows how, when or where they originated; and that they are worthless.

2. As against the second class of extremists, we know that there are traditions that carry us back to the times when, and to the places where, the facts happened, and that, consequently, are most reliable sources of information. Therefore, to treat all traditions alike and to assign to them all the *highest value,* or to assign to them all the *lowest,* or even *no, value* is entirely uncritical and unhistorical.

3. The fact is, that no general rule can be laid down as to the value of all mere human traditions in general, just as no general rule can be laid down as to the value of all writings in general. The prudent critic should determine the value of each tradition, as he comes to it; but to reject all traditions on principle and antecedently to every investigation is absurd.

Apropos of this question, the student will, no doubt, be pleased to read the moderate and judicious remarks of a non-Catholic professor of Scripture in one of our American institutions, Dr. A. C. Zenos, who writes: " But there are traditions and traditions. There are accounts of facts which were described accurately by eye witnesses and attested by signs of unmistakable good faith, [traditions] which were transmitted for a time orally and then written down. They differ very little, if at all, from first hand-written testimony. In fact the difference between these traditions and firsthand [written?] testimony is one of formal and not of essential nature. Some subjects have been under discussion from time immemorial, and traditions regarding them have been tested and verified by each successive generation of students interested in them. Such traditions evidently gain in weight by each successive examination. Often the processes of examination may be lost, leaving no trace behind them; but succeeding generations of scholars, basing themselves on the well-known fact of the verification of these traditions by their predecessors, may accept them as true without hesitation. It is part of sound criticism to distinguish between traditions and traditions; to test each as it is met; to allow each its proper force and bearing upon the results of the investigation on hand. This diversity between different kinds of traditions will make an *a priori* stand on them, as a class, an altogether unscientific procedure." (*Elements of Higher Criticism*, pp. 148-149.)

Traditions, if such exist, should serve as the starting point in the investigations of the higher critic and, unless they are manifestly false on the face of them, the presumption favors them as being in possession, and they have the right to stand, until they have been shown to be false.

We do not have to prove that the traditions are right; we can take that for granted; for the *onus probandi* rests upon the critics to prove positively that they are wrong,— which they seldom succeed in doing (Whatley, *Rhetoric*.)

In such cases, also, the tradition may form a good working hypothesis, until it has been carefully examined and found wanting.

In conclusion, we may say that, not of course the fanatics, but many of the most candid and most learned scholars among Protestants are coming more and more to the conviction, and are compelled by the facts in the case to admit, that oral teaching was the only means chosen by Christ for the spread of the Gospel and that, committing a part of His teaching to writing was, as it were, only an after-thought, a later and secondary development.

Some of them go still further and acknowledge the necessity and the authority of divine tradition, and admit that the Catholic rule of faith and the Catholic principle of hermeneutics are the rule and the principle of the Christian Church.

Even Luther acknowledges this truth when he says: " We are obliged to yield many things to the Papists; for instance, that with them is the word of God, which we receive from them, otherwise we should have known nothing at all about it." (Comment on John, Chap 16.)

Collier says. " Without tradition we can not prove that either the Old or the New Testament contains the word of God." (Haeninghaus, *La Réforme contre la Réforme*, C. V.)

Grotius says: " Above all, it must be taken for granted that everything which is generally adopted, without our being able to discover its origin, comes from the Apostles " (*Votum pro Pace,* p 137 )

Lessing says · " It is tradition and not Scripture on which the Church of Christ is built." " All antiquity speaks in favor of tradition with a voice which our reformers have too much slighted. They ought to have allowed to tradition, at least tradition such as Irenaeus understood it, the same divine authority, as they see fit to allow exclusively to Scripture." Then, in reply to those who object that tradition can be falsified, he says: " If tradition can be falsified, can not the Sacred Books also have been falsified? "

Dr. Westcott, sometime Professor at Oxford, Anglican Bishop of Durham, and one of the most learned men of his day, says: " The Apostles nowhere claim to give in writing a system of Christian doctrine. . . . Their teaching was by word of mouth and it never was their intention to create a permanent literature." (*The Bible in the Church,* pp 52–61.)

Dr. A. C Headlam expressly says: " It is impossible to limit our authority for Christianity to the Bible. . . . The controversy between the authority of Christian tradition and the authority of Christian Scripture is unprofitable, for the antithesis is a false one [*i.e.,* the pretended opposition of the one to the other does not exist]. The Scriptures are simply a part of the tradition of the Church." *(History, Authority and Theology,* 1909, pp. 71–72.)

Dr Porteus writes: " No one will deny that Jesus Christ laid the foundation of the Church by preaching. Nor can we deny that the unwritten Word or tradition was the first rule of Christianity" *(Comparative View)*.

But if tradition was the first rule of Christianity, it is still the *first* and the *last* and the *only* rule of Christianity; for no change ever has been or ever can be made. It is the will of Christ that it should be so. No one has the right or the might to change it for all time. What He has willed is good enough for the Catholic Church.

# PART III

# HOW TO EXPLAIN TO OTHERS THE SENSE OF SCRIPTURE

# CHAPTER VII

## DEFINITION

Exegesis, in general, may be defined as an explanation, explication, exposition, or interpretation of a writing in the broadest sense of those words. Hermeneutics is the science of interpretation; exegesis is the interpretation itself. Hermeneutics is the *theory* of interpretation; exegesis is the reduction of that theory to *practice*. It is applied hermeneutics.

There is this difference between exegesis and higher criticism: exegesis explains the meaning of a book; that is, it explains that thought which the author had in his mind and which he wished to communicate to his readers by means of written language. This is exegetical or subjective truth.

Higher criticism seeks to determine the intrinsic value of that meaning, and to decide whether it is true and reliable in itself and whether it has an independent existence apart from the author. If so, this is objective truth.

### Kinds of Exegesis

There are many kinds of exegesis, which differ from one another only in regard to the *subject-matter* or the topics which they handle; such as legal, historical, scientific, philosophical, theological, Biblical exegesis.

This last is general exegesis, applied, with certain modifications and additions, to the Bible. Biblical exegesis is of three kinds:

(1) The translation;
(2) The paraphrase;
(3) The commentary.

These three varieties of exegesis differ, not in the *subject-matter,* but in the *method* which they follow in handling any one book.

All three forms of exegesis may be adopted by the same writer and in the same work, as was done by Piconius in his famous *Triple Exposition of St. Paul's Epistles,* and every good commentary will at least try to combine the advantages to be derived from all the three modes of exegesis.

(1) *Translation*

The translation or version is the reproduction of the exact words of a writing in a language different from the original. There are chiefly two kinds of translation, (1) the literal, (2) the free.

The *literal* translation is the reproduction in another language of the *exact words* of the original, with exactly the *same meaning* and, as far as may be, with the *same number* and the *same order* of words, and with the *same construction* of sentences, as in the original It is made for the use of scholars and may serve as a basis for critical work.

The *free* translation, while reproducing faithfully the *thought* of the original, should conform to the genius, and should adopt the idioms, of the language into which it is made. It is intended for popular use and for public reading and should aim at elegance, but not at the expense of accuracy.

The translation simply takes a book out of one language and puts it into another; nothing more, nothing less. It should *add* nothing, it should *take away* nothing, it should *change* nothing, in the book,— except the language.

It should reproduce the original, just as it is, without attempting to *correct,* to *improve,* or in any way to *modify* it. Even the ambiguities and the obscurities of the original should be faithfully reproduced in the version; also the literary form, such as prose and poetry, figures of speech, rhythm, verse, the entire physiognomy, as far as the linguistic idioms and the genius of the language will permit.

The requisites of a good translation are principally these three: (1) fidelity, (2) clearness, (3) elegance.

Of these the most important is fidelity, the least important is elegance.

## (2) *The Paraphrase*

The paraphrase is a reproduction or restatement of the author's thought in *other* and *clearer words* and in *greater detail,* than in the original. Paraphrase is translation *with latitude,* it is a rendering of the sense in ample terms, in more and different words.

The paraphrase is a simple development of the text, retaining, as far as possible, the same words and phrases, but adding others to make the sense clear, to complete the thought, to indicate the connection of parts, and to show the relation of the ideas to one another.

Unlike the translation, the paraphrase may, and sometimes should, *add* or *take away words,* when necessary to make the sense clearer than before. Vague and ambiguous terms should be replaced by words of *precise* and *definite meaning.* Obscure facts should be explained by reference to history or archaeology, and words evidently omitted and understood should be inserted to complete the sense or to show the logical sequence of ideas. A good paraphrase should be: (1) faithful, (2) transparent, (3) brief.

### (3) *The Commentary in General*

The word commentary is taken either (1) in a broad or (2) in a narrow sense.

In its *broad* sense, a commentary is an explanation of a writing, distinct from the writing itself. In this general sense, the commentary includes such varieties as: (a) the gloss, (b) the scholion, (c) the annotation, (d) the homily, (e) the dissertation exegetical, (f) the commentary in the strict and proper sense of the word. We shall explain them in order.

### a) *The Gloss*

The *gloss,* which is the earliest and the simplest form of exegesis, is a short note or comment explaining the meaning of some rare, obsolete, or foreign *word* in a classical or Biblical text.

The term was first applied to the word that *needed*

explanation, but soon came to mean the word that *gave* the explanation,— and that is the present meaning of the word.

With time the gloss developed from the explanation of mere *words* to the examination of grammatical *constructions* and then to the discussion of the *subject-matter* of the book.

Centuries ago glosses were gathered together in alphabetic order into what were called glossaries,— the beginning of our modern dictionaries.

### b) *The Scholion*

The scholion is a short note or remark intended to explain some obscure or difficult *word* or *phase* or *topic* in a text.

The gloss and the scholion were first used in the classical writings of Greece and Rome and then applied to the text of Sacred Scripture.

The glossator and the scholiast are interpreters of *single detached words or topics,* and not expounders of the continuous *collective thought* of the author. They have to do with separate, individual words or topics and explain them, much as the dictionary explains single words.

The gloss and the scholion are written either in the margin, or between the lines, or at the foot of the page, and were never intended to make a part of the text. When, inadvertently or otherwise, the copyist allowed them to creep into the text, it became the task of the textual critic to eliminate them.

### c) *The Annotation*

The words gloss and scholion are now seldom used unless historically and in speaking of the past. They have been replaced by the word *annotation*.

The annotation also is a short remark or a critical comment on the text of Sacred Scripture. It has *widened out* the sphere of usefulness of the gloss and the scholion, and is used to explain matters of a grammatical, lexical, historical, archaeological, dogmatic or ascetic nature; used also to harmonize apparently discrepant statements of the author; to unravel exegetical difficulties, or to clear up doctrinal problems. The annotation is preferred by many students of Sacred Scripture, as less tedious than the commentary.

It is neither easy nor necessary to define rigorously or to discriminate nicely the various shades of meaning of these words. In general, the gloss is more *verbal;* the scholion is more *real;* the annotation is both, but more ample and varied. They are all restricted to the more *difficult* parts of the text and are shorter and less continuous than the commentary proper, from which they differ in *quantity*, not in *quality;* in *bulk,* not in *kind.*

### d) *The Homily*

The *homily* is a didactic, popular, and practical discourse explaining some text of Sacred Scripture and applying it to the spiritual needs of the people, to their instruction and edification. The homily is addressed to the intellect and to the will, to the head and

## HOW TO EXPLAIN SCRIPTURE 177

to the heart. It was the only kind of preaching known for centuries to the early Church and was practiced by Origin, Chrysostom, Augustine, Gregory the Great, and many others. It may be in writing or may be delivered orally to the people. This latter is the homily proper.

We may discuss the homily either homiletically or hermeneutically, because it is both a *popular discourse* and it is also an *explanation* of a Bible text. The principles of *homiletics* will tell how the homily is to be composed and delivered, in order to produce the proper oratorical effect on the people. The principles of hermeneutics will tell how the homily should be composed, in so far as it is an exposition of a text of Sacred Scripture

In the choice of material for the homily, subtle distinctions, philosophical speculations, chronological or philological disquisitions and the conflicting opinions of philosophers and scientists soon weary and disgust our people, many of whom, if they could, might go to college for such things, but they go to church for something better,— to church, where " the poor have the Gospel preached to them " Instead of wearying them with abstract, intricate, complicated problems, use similitudes, use figures of speech, use apt illustrations, use pertinent examples and concrete facts, and they will be both better *instructed* and more permanently *edified*.

As to the disposition of such materials, an orderly arrangement, a logical sequence of ideas, and a consecutiveness in the major and even in the minor divisions of the discourse (in which each step prepares the way for the next step) are essential to clearness and are felt and appreciated by even an uneducated audience. They know, as well as he does, when the preacher is floundering.

The style of language in the homily should be neither involved nor complicated, but *open, simple, straightforward* and such, both in *words* and in *structure,* that all may be readily understood. If managed properly, such a style may be both most beautiful and most attractive.

As to the manner of explaining the text, the homilist should remember that he is a commentator and should discuss the subject accordingly, with the restrictions given above.

### e) *The Exegetical Dissertation*

The *exegetical dissertation* may be *defined* as a systematic and argumentative interpretation, a thoroughgoing, and exhaustive exposition of some one text or passage of Sacred Scripture, short but important, and discussed in all its bearings. Briefly, it is a *large* commentary on a *small* text.

It is not generically Biblical, but specifically *exegetical* It is a commentary pure and simple and, therefore, should follow all the methods and should possess all the requisites of the commentary, except brevity. It is intended to be full and exhaustive, and should leave nothing unsaid

Such questions as the primacy of Peter, the Virgin Birth, divorce, the eschatology and Christology of Paul, the Resurrection of Christ, etc., are frequent themes for exegetical dissertation.

# HOW TO EXPLAIN SCRIPTURE 179

Such dissertations are often placed at the end of commentaries, as supplements or appendixes, when a thorough exposition of some important passages, if left in the body of the work, would be out of proportion to the size of the commentary. The requisites of a good exegetical dissertation are (1) sincerity, (2) clearness, and (3) completeness.

### f) *The Commentary Proper*

The Biblical commentary proper, in the strict and *narrow* sense of the word, is a *systematic, complete,* and *continuous* explanation of the meaning of a Bible text, distinct from the text itself, and developed by comment, remark, observation, criticism, or by any other means that will explain it to others.

In order to discover the true sense of a writing and to prove by arguments that it *is* the true sense, and to explain properly that sense to others, the commentator may, if he can, avail himself of all branches of human knowledge, such as philology, logic, history, geography, archaeology, philosophy, theology, and the natural sciences.[1]

The commentary (in all its varieties) differs essentially from the translation and from the paraphrase in this, that the translator and the paraphrast impersonate the author, identify themselves with the author and speak in the name of the *author*,— speak from within

[1] "In the exegesis of the various sections, for the purpose of elucidating obscure passages, the commentator must avail himself of all the resources of scholarship in the domain of philology, history and theology, and also use his own opinions, provided always that he attends to the fundamental principles of the Church." (Seisenberger, *Practical Handbook*, page 471.)

and through his text: whereas the commentator speaks in his *own* name and from *outside* the *text* and gives his own personal opinion about the meaning of the text.

Thus the translation and the paraphrase are, in a sense, identical with the text. They are the text, though in another dress and in a slightly different form.

On the other hand the commentary, as said in the above definition, "is *distinct* from the text." There are such strange things as commentaries on the text without the text. In such cases, the student needs to have near at hand a copy of the Bible for ready reference to the text. In such cases, too, the commentary is not only "distinct from the text," but also *separate* from the text.

## Requisites of a Good Commentary

As every student of Scripture is expected, not indeed to write, but to study commentaries, he should know a good one when he sees it.

A good commentary may be known, (1) partly by what *precedes* and (2) partly by what *accompanies* it.

A good commentary should be *preceded* by a prolegomenon, or special introduction to the particular book to be commented.

Such prolegomenon should contain (unless already given elsewhere) a short *biographical sketch* of the author to be commented, showing who and what he was, when and where he lived, and how and why, and for what specific purpose and on what occasion and

## HOW TO EXPLAIN SCRIPTURE 181

on what topics and for what special class of readers he wrote[1]

It should show also the general *tenor* or *drift* of the book; it should give a sufficiently detailed analysis of its principal *doctrinal, moral,* and *historical* contents; also the author's *favorite teachings,* the peculiarities of his *style* and *diction,* and any other facts or data that might be of special interest to the student of the book

If such information is given systematically and in logical order, it can be given very *briefly,* yet *fully,* and will be of incalculable advantage to the student, enabling him to run away with the commentary in one half the time that would otherwise be needed and with results much more permanent and in every way more satisfactory than could otherwise be obtained.

During the *course* of the commentary the following mistakes should be avoided:

1) Some commentators forget to give an *analysis* of each chapter.

2) Some give only their own interpretation of important passages and neglect to mention the divergent and, perhaps, better interpretation of the great commentators of the past.[2]

[1] "The actual commentary is preceded by an introduction to the book, discussing the author and the readers for whom he wrote, the motive, purpose and contents of the book, and the place and date of its composition. In this way the reader is supplied with a preliminary survey of the book, is enabled to form some opinion regarding it, and is prepared to understand its various parts" (Seisenberger, *Practical Handbook,* page 471.)

[2] "Finally we expect of a commentator that he should mention the chief explanations put forward by others with whom he does not agree, giving at the same time his reasons for refusing to assent to them." (Seisenberger, *Practical Handbook,* page 471)

3) Some, in their hurry, misinterpret the opinions of other commentators.

4) Some give as certain what is only probable.

5) Some indulge in long digressions, which might better be given as dissertations or supplements at the end of the volume or of the chapter.

6) Some pay undue attention to minute details, grammatical, lexical, historical, and thus obscure the main issue,— the general tenor of the book as a whole.

7) Some lose time and weary the reader in rehearsing the antiquated, in emphasizing the obvious, and in accumulating proofs for what nobody denies or for what is of little moment; while, at the same time, they display a truly marvelous skill in steering clear of passages of prime importance or touching them only superficially, for no other reason, apparently, than because they are difficult to handle.

The requisites of a good commentary are (1) sincerity, (2) clearness, and (3) brevity.

*Kinds of Commentary*

As exegesis gives large play to the individuality of the commentator, his work will vary very much in character and form, according to the aim he has in view, and will correspond to the needs of the theologian, the pastor, or the people. As to commentaries proper we need speak of only the following three kinds:

(1) The philological, or grammatico-historical;

(2) The theological, or dogmatic-moral;

(2) The pastoral, or homiletical and practical.

A few words will suffice to explain them.

### 1) *Philological Exegesis*

The *philological* or grammatico-historical exegesis of Scripture, as the name implies, is concerned with *verbal minutiae,* with critical discussions as to the exact meaning of the words of the Sacred Text, when judged according to the grammar and the lexicon of the language used. Each word must be examined etymologically and historically and its meaning not only ascertained, but demonstrated. This serves as a *basis* for all sound and scientific exposition of Scripture. The original text, Hebrew for the Old and Greek for the New Testament, is used in this kind of exegesis. It should also be borne in mind that there are certain *grammatical, rhetorical* and *logical* features that are quite peculiar to ancient Biblical literature. These should not be overlooked by the exegete. Prose should be distinguished from poetry, each kind of prose from every other kind, historical, legal, oratorical, etc.; and each kind of poetry from every other kind, epic, lyric, etc., and all these, as we find them in the Bible, from the non-Biblical. St. Jerome excels in this kind of commentary.

### 2) *Theological Exegesis*

The *theological* or dogmatic and moral exegesis develops the *doctrinal* and *ethical* sense of the text according to the sense of the Church, the consensus of the Fathers, and the analogy of Catholic faith. This kind of commentary often transcends, though it does not contradict, the rules of Hebrew grammar, the definitions of the Hebrew lexicon, the rules of rhetoric and the laws of logic. It is based on *divine revelation.* The sense of the Holy Ghost, the primary author of Sacred Writ, is often deeper than the letter of the text, and sometimes quite escaped the mental grasp of the ancient prophet of Israel. This is true especially of all the mysteries, of the Messianic predictions, and of the mystical sense in general. The Latin Vulgate should be used, but by no means to the exclusion of the original text or of the ancient versions, officially authenticated by the mere fact that the Church has adopted them for use in her Oriental liturgies. St. Augustine excels in this kind of commentary.

In regard to the use of the Scriptures in the study of both *dogmatic* and *moral* theology, Pope Leo XIII tells us some very primitive truths, but all the more necessary, especially at a time when some seem to forget that the Bible is one of the two principal channels of revealed truth and allow the study of it to fall into comparative neglect He says in his encyclical " *Providentissimus ":* " It is most essential and most desirable that the whole teaching of theology should be pervaded and animated by the use of the divine written Word of God. The Sacred Books hold such an eminent place among the sources of revelation that, without the constant study and use of them, theology cannot be placed on its true footing. Without divine revelation there is no way left to prove the articles of faith by reason alone; we can only solve the difficulties raised against them; for theology does not receive her first principles from any other science, but immediately from God, by revelation."

From these words we may infer that the study of Sacred Scripture is of primary importance in any course of ecclesiastical studies. In fact, unless theology refreshes its life by repeated draughts from this fountain of pure doctrine, it is in danger of languishing, and of crystallizing into lifeless systems and schools; which soon outlive their usefulness.

### 3) *Homiletical or Practical Exegesis*

The *homiletical* or practical exegesis is the application of the revelation contained in Scripture to the spiritual needs of the people. It is *made with a view to the pulpit*, but must be based on the two preceding kinds of exegesis. But it goes beyond them, in so far as it gives the practical application of the text to the matter in hand. The exegete digs out of Holy Writ the nuggets of solid gold which the preacher moulds into the current coin of the day. Here the professor in his chair is of practical assistance to the preacher in the pulpit. The final aim of all Biblical study, the goal to which all naturally tends, is the instruction and edification of the faithful. Not to reach this end, is to stop on the way. St. John Chrysostom excels in this kind of commentary.

More, if possible, in homiletics than in theology, the same Holy Father so much insists on the necessity of quoting Sacred Writ abundantly, while preaching to the people. He says: "There is in Holy Scripture a singular power, which gives authority to the sacred orator, fills him with apostolic liberty of speech, and communicates force and energy to his eloquence." He severely reproves those preachers "who use no words but those of human science and human prudence, trusting to their own reasonings rather than to those of God. Such preaching is feeble and cold. " For the word of God is living and effectual, and more piercing than a two-edge sword, and reaching into the division of the soul and the spirit. It is an overflowing fountain of salvation, a fertile pasture, a beautiful garden, in which the flock of the Lord is marvellously refreshed and delighted."

# APPENDIX

# APPENDIX

## SOME RESULTS OF EXEGESIS [1]

Among the sciences which result from exegesis are Biblical theology, Biblical history, Biblical biography, etc.

*Biblical Theology.*—In its modern technical sense, Biblical theology is a *systematic presentation* of the *doctrinal* and *ethical* truths scattered up and down through the entire range of Holy Scripture. It sums up all the results of exegesis and groups them under proper headings for convenience of reference and for study. The truths revealed in Scripture are not there labeled and put away in their respective places as curiosities in a museum, but are scattered about the Bible in the wildest profusion without order or method, like objects in nature, like flowers in a forest. Biblical theology arranges them according to some system.

*Biblical History.*—As Scripture teaches many of its moral lessons by the providential events of the religious and the political history of God's chosen people, another result of exegesis is the "History of Israel," as found in the Old Testament and the "History of the Apostolic Church," as found in the Acts of the Apostles and also in the Epistles of the New Testament.

[1] We mention this subject here, though ever so briefly, in order to round out and complete the outline of Biblical studies.

*Biblical Biography.*—Again, as Scripture teaches chiefly by the concrete object lessons exemplified in the lives of the saints and martyrs of the Good Book, another result of the exegesis is that the study of Biblical biography has resuscitated from the pages of the sacred volume a Moses, a David, an Isaias, an Evangelist John, an Apostle Paul, and systematically relates of them all that can now be known.

But the gem of them all is the *Life of Christ.* This is the kernel of all Scripture. Some interpreters never get beyond the dry-as-chaff details of grammar and lexicon, and never reach the contents of the Sacred Volume, never get the spirit. " They only gnaw at the bark, but never reach the pith." What is the pith of Scripture?

Jesus Christ is the pith of Scripture. He is the centre, the life, the soul, the substance of the written Word of God. The Incarnate Word of God pervades and imparts life to the written Word. Him we must seek in Scripture, and Him we must preach to the people.

Pope Leo XIII expresses this truth in beautiful language: " Nowhere is there anything more fully or more clearly expressed in regard to the Saviour of the World than is to be found in the entire range of the Bible. St. Jerome says, ' To be ignorant of the Scriptures, is to be ignorant of Jesus Christ.' In its pages the image of Christ stands out living and breathing and diffusing everywhere around consolation in trouble, encouragement to virtue, and attraction to the love of God " (Encyclical *Providentissumus Deus*).

Holy Scripture is, indeed, pregnant with Christ

*(" Lex gravida Christo ").* In Genesis He is mentioned for the first time, but only as the " seed of the woman." From this protevangelium, from this rudimentary beginning, we can trace, throughout the entire Old Testament, the gradual development of this idea; we can everywhere see the image of a marvellous man, gentle yet awful, near yet distant as the unseen God; a man described by the prophets of Israel with ever-increasing accuracy of detail, until, at the appointed time, prediction is fulfilled in the " Word made flesh," is realized in the Infant in the stable of Bethlehem, and in the divine Rabbi of Nazareth, who drew aside the veil of prophecy and stood before the world in the garb of human nature, and in the dignity and majesty of God.

The Bible is to all other books what heaven is to earth, so far is it above them all. It has heights and depths of thought reaching into the infinite. It is full of the mysteries of time and eternity, of God and man, of heaven and earth, of life and death, of sin and grace, of struggles, defeats and victories. It is so simple, in parts, that children can understand it; so profound in parts that an Augustine can not fathom it.

It speaks of God in a thousand ways: through dogma, moral law, ethics, philosophy, history and biography; in prose and poetry; in psalms, hymns, and canticles; in sacrifices and sacraments; in the pillar of fire and in the cloud; in allegories and parables; in dreams, visions, theophanies, and prophecies,— all so many golden links in the long chain of the divine self-revelation of God, extending down through the ages and terminating in the last great Theophany in which the " Word of God," the Revealer and the Revealed, appeared in the flesh and " dwelt among us, and we saw His glory, the glory of the only-begotten Son of God, full of grace and truth."

# BIBLIOGRAPHY

# BIBLIOGRAPHY

Besides the general works listed in Volume I the student may consult:

ARIGLER, Altman. *Hermeneutica Biblica Generalis;* Vienna, 1913, 1 Vol.
BAINVEL, J. V. *De Magisterio Vivo et Traditione;* Paris, 1905.
BÉGIN, Cardinal. *The Rule of Faith:* tr., London, 1910.
BILLOT, Card. L. *De Inspiratione S. S.;* Rome, 1906.
BILLOT, Card. L. *De Immutabilitate Traditionis;* Rome, 1907.
BONACCORSI, G. *L'Interpretazione della Scrittura Secundo la Dottrina Cattolica;* Bologna, 1904.
BRANDI, S. M. *La Questione Biblica;* Rome, 1894.
BRUCKER, J. *Questions Actuelles d' Ecriture Sainte;* Paris, 1 Vol, 1895.
BRUCKER, J *L'Etendue de L'Inspiration;* Paris, 1895.
BRUNEAU, J. *On Biblical Inspiration; Amer. Eccles. Review,* March, 1896.
CASEY, P. H. *The Bible and Its Interpreters;* Philadelphia, 1911.
CHAUVIN, C. *Introduction Generale; Hermeneutique;* Section V, pp. 435-624.
DAVIDSON, Samuel. *Sacred Hermeneutics and History of Biblical Interpretation;* Edinburgh, 1843.
DIDIOT, J. *Traite de la S. Écriture d' Après Leon XIII,* Paris, 1894
DURAND, A *Inerrance, Inspiration* in *Dict. Apol.,* t. II, 752-787, 894-912.
EGGER, P. M *Absolute oder relative wahrheit der hl. schrift;* Brixen, 1909.
ERNESTI, J. A. *Institutio Interpretis New Testamenti;* Leipzig, 1761. Still useful.
FAIRBAIRN, Patrick. *Hermeneutical Manual; Introduction to the Study of the New Testament;* Edinburgh & Phila., 1859
FILLON, L. *Les Étapes du Rationalisme centre les Evangiles;* Paris, 1 Vol., 1911.

## BIBLIOGRAPHY

Fonck, L. *Der Kampf um die Wahrheit der hl. Schrift;* Innsbruck, 1905
Fonsgrive, G. L. *L'Attitude du Catholique devant la Science;* Paris, 1900.
Franzelin, Card. *Tractatus de Divina Traditione et S. S.;* Rome, 1875
Gigot, F. E. *General Introduction;* Interpretation, Chaps. XVI–XIX, pp 382–467
Guentner, G H. *Hermeneutica Biblica Generalis;* 1 Vol., Prague, 1863.
Hurst. *History of Rationalism;* New York, 1865.
Jacquier, E. *The New Testament in the Christian Church,* Paris, 4 Vol.
Janssens, J. H. *Hermeneutica Sacra;* Mainz, 1818 2 vol., 8vo.
Kohlgruber, J. *Hermeneutica Biblica Generalis,* Vienna, 1850.
Milner, John. *The End of Religious Controversy;* 1 Vol.; numerous editions in all shapes, styles and sizes
Patrizzi, S. J. *De Interpretatione S Scripturae;* Freiburg
Ranolder, J *Hermeneuticae Generalis Principia Rationalia Christiana et Catholica;* Leipzig, 1839
Reitmayer, F. X. *Lehrbuch der Biblischen Hermeneutik;* Kempten, 1874.
Terry, M. S. *Biblical Hermeneutics;* 1 Vol, New York, 1911.
Unterkircher, C. *Hermeneutica Biblica;* Innsbruck, 1854.
Vigouroux-Brassac. *Manuel Biblique;* Hermeneutique, pp. 235–272

If the student wishes to study the relative merits of the Catholic and the Protestant principles of Hermeneutics, he might consult:

1) Bégin, L. N. *The Bible and the Rule of Faith*
2) Mazella, Cardinal. *De Virtutibus Infusis;* no 889 sq.
3) Milner, J. *End of Religious Controversy;* Letters 5–12, inclusive
4) Murray, P. *De Ecclesia;* Vol III, Disputation XIV.
5) Perrone, Fr. *Il Protestantesimo e la Regola di Fede.*
6) Spalding, M J. *Evidences of Catholicity,* Lecture III.
7) Tanquery, Ad. *Synopsis Theologiae Fundamentalis;* pp. 363, 376
8) Wiseman, Cardinal. *Lectures on the Principal Doctrines and Practices of the Church,* Lectures II–III.

# BIBLIOGRAPHY

Of these writers some discuss the subject more theologically, others discuss it more hermeneutically. The result is about the same.

THE END

# INDEX

(The Roman numerals refer to the volume, the Arabic numerals to the pages)

Accommodated sense of Scripture, IV, 15 sq.; IV, 101 sqq.
Alphabet, I, 29.
Analogy of the faith, IV, 70 sqq.
Annotations, Scriptural, IV, 176
Apocryphal books, III, 151 sqq.
Aquila, I, 116 sq.
Archaeology, Biblical, V, 157 sqq.; Definition, V, 157 sq.; Scope, I, 158 sq.; Sources, II, 159; Results, II, 159 sqq.
"Authentic," meaning of the word as used by the Council of Trent, I, 165 sqq.
Authority in Scripture, II, 53 sqq.
"Authorized" Version, I, 191 sqq.

Beza, Th., II, 35.
Bible history, IV, 189.
Bible, The· Definition, I, 3; Names, I, 3 sqq.; Division, I, 5 sqq.; Importance and beauty of, I, 7 sqq.
Biblical Commission, III, 93 sqq., IV, 77 sqq.
Biography, Biblical, IV, 190 sq
Bishops' Bible, I, 190 sq.

Canon, Definition of, III, 145 sqq.; Kinds of canonical books, III, 148 sqq.; Apocryphal books, III, 151 sqq.; Criterion of canonization in O. T., III, 155 sq ; Inspiration and canonization, III, 156 sqq.; Of the O. T., III, 160 sqq.; Two canons, III, 161; Theories concerning formation of O. T. canon, III, 161 sqq.; History of the Palestinian canon, III, 164 sqq.; O. T. canon in the Christian Church, III, 183 sqq.; At the Council of Trent, III, 196 sq.; Among the sects, III, 197 sq.; Of the N. T., III, 199 sqq.; How collected, III, 203 sqq.; History, III, 209 sqq.; Muratorian fragment, III, 216 sqq.; The N. T. canon among Protestants, III, 227 sqq.
Challoner, I, 207
Church, The place of S. Scripture in the, IV, 154 sqq.
Codices. N. T., I, 79 sqq.; II, 16 sqq.
Commentary, Scriptural, IV, 174 sqq., 179 sqq.; Requisites of a good, IV, 180 sqq.; Kinds of, IV, 182 sqq
Context, as a criterion of interpretation, IV, 29 sq.

199

# INDEX

Coverdale, M., I, 189.
Crampon Version, I, 210.
Criteria of higher criticism, II, 105 sqq.; The internal literary criterion, II, 107 sqq.; The internal historical criterion, II, 112 sqq.; The internal theological criterion, II, 115 sqq.; The internal quotational criterion, II, 117 sqq; The negative external historical criterion, II, 121 sqq; The positive external historical criterion, II, 126 sqq.
Critics, Classes of, II, 84 sqq.; False postulates of, II, 128 sqq.
Criticism, II, 3 sqq.

Diatessaron, I, 102.
Dissertation, The exegetical, IV, 178 sq.
Douay or Rheims version, I, 198 sqq

Elzevir Brothers, II, 35 sq.
Erasmus, II, 34 sq.
Errors of transcription or translation, II, 7 sqq.
Esdras, I, 53; III, 169 sq, 173.
Eusebius, I, 121 sq
Exegesis, Scriptural, IV, 183 sqq, Some results of, IV, 189 sqq.

Families of N. T. MSS., II, 41 sqq.
Fathers, Quotations from the early, II, 26 sqq.

General Introduction to the Bible, Meaning of, I, xiii sqq.; Definition, I, xiii; Purpose, I, xiv sq.; Extent, I, xv sq.; General character, I, xvi sqq; Division, I, xviii; Necessity of, I, xviii sq.; Place of, I, xix sqq.
Geneva Bible, I, 190.
Genuineness of the Sacred Books, II, 58 sqq.
Graphe, III, 26 sqq.
Gloss, The, IV, 174 sq
Greek, Biblical, I, 34 sqq.

Hebrew, I, 27 sqq., I, 43 sqq.
Hermeneutics, Biblical, IV, 1 sqq.; Rational principles of, IV, 25 sqq.; Christian principles of, IV, 35 sqq.; Catholic principles of, IV, 47 sqq.; Protestant principles of, IV, 83 sqq., Rationalistic principles of, IV, 95 sqq.
Hesychius, I, 122.
Hexapla, I, 119 sq.
Higher Biblical Criticism, II, 46 sqq.; Province of, II, 51 sqq.; Definition of, I, 55 sqq.; As a science, II, 97 sqq.; Its principles and methods, II, 102 sqq; False postulates of, II, 128 sqq.
Homily, The, IV, 176 sqq.
Human authority of the Bible, II, 78 sqq.

Inerrancy of the Bible, III, 75 sq.
Infallibility of the Bible, III, 69 sqq.
Inspiration, III, 3 sqq; Criteria of, III, 6 sqq.; Proofs of, III, 22 sqq.; Of the O. T, III, 22 sqq.; Of the N. S., III, 31 sqq, Nature of, III, 37 sqq.; Definition of, III, 42 sqq.;

# INDEX

Verbal, III, 60 sqq , Extent of, III, 66 sqq , Effects of, III, 69 sqq., And science, III, 81 sqq , And history, III, 85 sqq , And quotations, III, 102 sqq , False theories of, III, 112 sqq ; Partial, III, 117 sqq.; As distinguished from revelation, III, 127 sqq ; Mechanical, III, 133 sqq ; Mystical, III, 136, Natural, III, 136 sqq , Inspiration and canonization, III, 156 sqq
"*Insuper,*" Decree, I, 149 sqq , I, 209 sq., IV, 50 sqq
Integrity of the Sacred Books, II, 65 sqq
Interpretation, Criteria of, IV, 28 sqq.
Itala, I, 123 sqq.

Jerome, St , I, 129 sqq.

Kenrick, F P , I, 208
King James Bible, I, 191 sqq.

Lachmann, C , II, 36 sq
Languages of the Bible, I, 13 sqq., Classes of, I, 16 sq ; Families of, I, 17 sqq.; Aryan, I, 22, Semitic, I, 23 sqq.
Latin translations of the Bible, The Itala, I, 123 sqq , The Vulgate, I, 128 sqq
Latin words in the Greek N T, I, 38
Leo XIII, III, 83 sq , 86 sq , 121 sqq., IV, 77; IV, 190.
Lingard, J , I, 208.
Literal sense of Scripture, IV, 8 sqq.
Literary form of the Bible, II, 71 sqq

Lucian, I, 122.
Luther, M , IV, 90, 165

McMahon, B , I, 208.
Massoretes I, 63 sqq.
Muratorian Canon, III, 216 sqq
Mystical sense of Scripture, IV, 11 sqq

Nary, C., I, 207 sq
Nehemias, I, 53
New Testament, Ancient MS. copies of, II, 16 sqq.; Printed editions, II, 33 sqq ; Families of N. T. MSS., II, 41 sqq ; History of the text of, I, 79 sqq ; Canon of, III, 199 sqq., 227 sqq.

Old Testament, Hebrew text of, I, 43 sqq , History of this text, I, 51 sqq ; Early printed editions, I, 71 sqq.
Origen, I, 119 sqq

Parallelism, Biblical, IV, 30 sq.
Paraphrase, The, IV, 173 sq.
Pentateuch, Samaritan, I, 71 sqq
Peshitto, I, 99 sqq
Pius X, IV, 78.
Poetry in the Bible, II, 75 sqq
Polyglot Bibles, I, 89 sq.
Postulates of radical criticism, II, 128 sqq
Private judgment in interpreting Scripture, IV, 85 sqq.

Quotations in the Bible, III, 102 sqq.

Rationalism, II, 87 sqq.; IV, 97 sqq.

# INDEX

Reading S. Scripture, I, 215 sqq.
Renan, E., II, 92, 94; IV, 112 sq
Revelation, As distinguished from inspiration, III, 127 sqq
Rogers, J., I, 189 sq.
Rules for determining which of various readings in the Greek N T. is the more correct, II, 30 sqq.

Scholion, The, IV, 175.
Scribes, I, 53 sqq
Semitic words in the N T., I, 36 sqq.
Sense of Scripture, IV, 7 sqq ; Literal, IV, 9 sqq , Typical or mystical, IV, 11 sqq.; Accommodated, IV, 15 sq.; How to discover, IV, 19 sqq.; How to explain, IV, 171 sqq.
Septuagint, I, 55, I, 67, I, 109 sqq.
Socinianism, IV, 95 sqq.
Spencer, A., I, 208 sq.
Stephanus, R , II, 35
Strauss, D. F , IV, 108 sqq.
Symmachus, I, 118.
Synopsis of Biblical Introduction, I, iii.

Talmudists, I, 62 sq
Tetrapla, I, 120.
Texts, Original, I, 43 sqq.
Textual criticism, I, 3 sqq.; Of the Hebrew O. T , II, 13 sq.; Of the Greek O T , II, 14 sq , Of the Greek N. T., II, 15 sqq
Theodotion, I, 117 sq.
Theology, Biblical, IV, 189.
Theopneustos, III, 28 sqq.
Tischendorf, C., II, 37.

Tradition, Of the Fathers, III, 34 sqq.; Divine, An essential part of the Catholic principle of hermeneutics, IV, 117 sqq ; Catholic doctrine of, IV, 134 sqq.
Tregelles, S P., II, 37.
Trent, Council of, I, 138 sqq.; III, 196 sq ; IV, 50 sqq.
Tyndale, W., I, 189.
Typical sense of Scripture, IV, 11 sqq.

*Usus loquendi,* Biblical, IV, 26 sqq

Various readings, II, 8 sqq , II, 30 sqq.
Versions of the Bible, Ancient, I, 95 sqq.; Oriental, I, 96 sqq., Aramaic, I, 97 sqq.; Syriac, I, 99 sqq ; Arabic, I, 103 sq ; Coptic, I, 104 sqq., Ethiopic, I, 106 sq ; Armenian, I, 106 sq ; Western versions, Gothic, I, 107 , Slavonic, I, 108 , Greek, I, 108 sqq.; Latin, I, 123 sqq.; Other Western versions, I, 186 sqq , Anglo-Saxon, I, 186 sqq ; English, I, 189 sqq ; French, I, 214; German, I, 214 sqq.; Ancient of the N T , II, 23 sqq.; Testimony of the ancient versions on the canon, III, 224 sqq
Virgin birth, The, II, 95
Vogels, H. J , II, 38 sqq
Vowel points in Hebrew O. T., I, 64 sqq
Vulgate, I, 128 sqq.

Westcott and Hort, II, 37 sq

Ximenes, Cardinal, I, 89; II, 34.

# BIBLIOLIFE

## Old Books Deserve a New Life
www.bibliolife.com

Did you know that you can get most of our titles in our trademark **EasyScript**™ print format? **EasyScript**™ provides readers with a larger than average typeface, for a reading experience that's easier on the eyes.

Did you know that we have an ever-growing collection of books in many languages?

Order online:
www.bibliolife.com/store

Or to exclusively browse our **EasyScript**™ collection:
www.bibliogrande.com

At BiblioLife, we aim to make knowledge more accessible by making thousands of titles available to you – quickly and affordably.

Contact us:
BiblioLife
PO Box 21206
Charleston, SC 29413

Printed in Great Britain
by Amazon